Why We Stayed
Honesty and Hope in the Churches of Christ

Benjamin J. Williams, editor

An Imprint of Sulis International
Los Angeles | London

WHY WE STAYED: HONESTY AND HOPE IN THE CHURCHES OF CHRIST

Copyright ©2018 by Benjamin J. Williams. All rights reserved. Except for brief quotations for reviews, no part of this book may be reproduced in any form or by any electronic or mechanical means, including information storage and retrieval systems, without written permission from the publisher. Email: info@sulisinternational.com.

Keledei Publications
An Imprint of Sulis International
Los Angeles | London

www.sulisinternational.com

Library of Congress Control Number: 2018936318
Paperback ISBN: 978-1-946849-19-9
eBook ISBN: 978-1-946849-18-2

Table of Contents

Preface i
Scot McKnight

Introduction 1
Benjamin J. Williams

I Stayed for the Restoration Plea 7
Everett Ferguson

I Stayed for the Love of Scripture 17
Jeremie Beller

I Stayed for the Christ in the Church of Christ 31
Matthew Dowling

I Stayed for the Charity 49
Steven C. Hunter

I Stayed for the Water 61
Grant B. Sullivan

I Stayed for the Table 77
Scott Elliott

I Stayed for the Singing 91
Benjamin J. Williams

I Stayed for the Wild Democracy 103
John Mark Hicks

I Stayed for the Wedding 121
Chris Altrock

I Stayed for the Light 137
Ron Highfield

I Stayed to Bloom Where I Am Planted 151
John Wilson

I Stayed for the Inheritance 163
Chris Rosser

Preface

No Perfect Christians, No Perfect Churches

There is no perfect church because every church is made up of entirely imperfect people. That also means there is no such thing as a perfect denomination, ahem, excuse me, perfect affiliation of churches like the Churches of Christ. Why? Because no matter how close to the ideal a specific church gets, no matter how close to the gold standard a group of churches gets to that standard, this side of glory that church and those churches will never be perfect. Your church, your group of churches, or your affiliation of churches then will never be the ideal form of the church or churches. Not until glory, and we're not there yet.

The wisest remark I ever read about churches was written by Dietrich Bonhoeffer. During the roar of Hitler's demonic capturing of the German Lutheran church—a sickening mix of Lutheranism, German culture, and Nazi power—Bonhoeffer said this:

> Every idealized human image that is brought into the Christian community is a hindrance to genuine community and must be broken up so that genuine community can survive. Those who love their dream of a Christian community more than the Christian community itself become destroyers of that Christian community even though their personal intentions may be ever so honest, earnest, and sacrificial…

He continues:

> Those who dream of this idealized community demand that it be fulfilled by God, by others, and by themselves.

What then is the alternative? Grace, even if it is costly grace, the answer is grace. The grace that comes to us in Christ and only in that grace in Christ are we connected in our fellowships. Bonhoeffer observes that our connection then looks like this: "we enter into that life together with other Christians, not as those who make demands, but as those who thankfully receive."[1] Only when we know we have received grace in Christ and therefore receive one another as fellow recipients of that grace do we comprehend what it means to be a church.

As an outsider to the Churches of Christ and as an admirer and friend to many in this tribe of Christians, I want to say two things: First, too many in the tradition have made demands and have lived in light of what Bonhoeffer calls an "idealized image." You know it and I know it, and it has at times wrecked local churches. But, second, I see a new spirit poured out among many Churches of Christ leaders, preachers, and congregants: a spirit of casting aside that idealized image and learning to live into the reality of what devoted, dedicated Christians actually do accomplish this side of glory. It's not the ideal, but it is at times breathtaking. It is not perfect, but the very imperfections at times reveal the glory of the power of the gospel at work in the Churches of Christ. It is not glory itself, but it is at times glorious.

This book is a collection of stories of those upon whom this new spirit is being poured out. Yes, it is the Spirit of God awakening many in the Churches of Christ that God wants faithfulness, not perfection; that God wants biblically-based churches that never become heaven itself; that God wants people to stick it out with one another. For in the sticking it out with one another, the true nature of the church becomes manifest to our world: ordinary people following Jesus together this side of glory who witness to the grace of God both by their obedience and their confessions of sins.

---

[1] Dietrich Bonhoeffer, *Life Together and Prayerbook of the Bible*, ed. Eberhard Bethge, trans. G.L. Müller, Dietrich Bonhoeffer Works 5 (Minneapolis: Fortress, 1996), 36.

Preface

This book, then, told me the deepest and truest story I've seen yet of the Churches of Christ. I'm glad to be what Mike Cope sometimes calls me: an honorary member.

Scot McKnight
Julius R. Mantey Professor of New Testament
Northern Seminary
Lisle, Illinois

Introduction

Imagine a spectrum of thought fixed between two books.

At one end of the spectrum might be Leroy Brownlow's *Why I Am a Member of the Church of Christ*.[1] It is a concise statement of the posture of the Church of Christ at its time and to a large degree even our own era. It describes this entity called the Church of Christ as a direct product of the Biblical text. The word "Scriptural" or "Bible" appears in fourteen out of twenty-five chapter headings and could easily be inserted into the rest. For Brownlow, the issue is plain: "The church of Christ was founded by Christ and the gates of hades shall not prevail against it; but other plants will be rooted up."[2] That the book is presently in its fifty-ninth printing since 1945 indicates a consensus among our people.

At the other end of the spectrum we might find *Why They Left*, edited by Flavil Yeakley.[3] This text acknowledges that the identity for the Church of Christ asserted by Brownlow has been difficult to maintain on the applied level. A movement begun for unity in Christ has all too often descended into a splintered fellowship squabbling over doctrinal differences. In the text, the usual suspects crop up: instrumental music, gender roles, divorce and remarriage, and more. In each case, the frustration of those making exodus from us seems to be that the Church of Christ either does not live up to its ideal or else has an ideal that cannot or should not be pursued. The book is a mere sampling of the frustration that

---

[1] Leroy Brownlow, *Why I Am a Member of the Church of Christ* (Fort Worth, TX: The Brownlow Corporation, 2011).

[2] Brownlow, 9.

[3] Flavil Ray Yeakley, *Why They Left: Listening to Those Who Have Left Churches of Christ* (Nashville, TN: Gospel Advocate Company, 2012).

has led many bright minds and faithful hearts out of our doors and pulpits.

In between these poles, we hope to place this book. This text even in its title, *Why We Stayed,* reflects both a sympathetic recognition of the frustrations that have driven some away and at the same time an abiding affection for the Church of Christ to which we each consider ourselves indebted. The authors of this text, to use a helpful paragraph from Allen and Hughes,

> ...see our family with clearer eyes. We see how it nourished us with love and instruction, and we learn to feel deep gratitude. But we also see ways it fell short and perhaps harmed us, and we feel regrets. We do not, for that reason, renounce our family. Rather we seek growth or reconciliation."[4]

The goal of this text is to communicate this sentiment to others. To the settled member reading Brownlow, we offer the discomfort of knowing that ours is not a perfect movement. To the injured soul who feels drawn more to the escape hatch, we offer the comfort of knowing that ours is a movement worth continuing, reforming, and preserving.

The contributors of this text are certainly an eclectic cast. The authors come from all parts of the Church of Christ spectrum, from conservative churches to progressive ones, whatever those terms might now mean. Some are in local church ministry and others are in the academic world. Some are young and only beginning their careers, while others are seasoned veterans with a lifetime of experience on which to reflect. It is no overstatement to say that we may only have two things in common. First, we all agree that the Church of Christ in our time has many blemishes. Second, we all agree that the virtues of the Church of Christ are still needed in this world. Beyond that, the reader will notice that our reasoning and approach to topics vary widely and wildly. The conviction shared by this cast of contributors is that the conversation being presented in this book needs to be voiced for the health of our own people.

---

[4] Crawford Leonard Allen and Richard T. Hughes, *Discovering Our Roots: The Ancestry of Churches of Christ* (Abilene, TX: ACU Press, 1988), 5.

Introduction

The first chapter comes from Everett Ferguson. When approached about this project, Dr. Ferguson responded with enthusiasm, but regretted to tell us that at this stage in his life he was no longer taking on new writing projects. However, he offered that should he answer the question of "why I stayed," it would sound a lot like his chapter on the Restoration plea in his previously published text, *The Early Church and Today, Volume 2*.[5] With his kind permission, that chapter is reprinted here. As he states, "The validity of the restoration concept is the crucial question of the raison d'être of churches of Christ." If the plea is reasonable and practical, then so to a large degree is the Church of Christ.

The second chapter is authored by Jeremie Beller, a minister who also works in the academy, focusing largely on homiletics. Beller points toward the commitment of our people to Scripture as a redeeming feature. It is the "stable ground in the midst of upheaval encountered by each generation." While he acknowledges the shortcomings of our approach to Scripture, Beller reminds us how wonderful it is to belong to a people committed to the text.

The third chapter comes from Matt Dowling. Dowling is a pulpit minister with an academic interest in the theological and historical roots of our movement among the Puritans. His contribution identifies the struggle to identify what the Church of Christ is all about. What is our center, and how do we articulate that center? As a decidedly non-confessional movement of free-spirited, autonomous congregations, what binds us together? Dowling offers in his chapter a proposal for doctrinal triage, allowing our identity to be tied to the essential elements of the ancient church and its earliest creeds.

Chapter four comes from Steven Hunter, a minister with a passion for church history. He reminds us of one of the great Restoration mottos: "in all things charity." This moral element of our hermeneutic and practice leads away from the hairsplitting found in too many pulpits toward a more loving spirit of brotherhood. Hunter believes this motto, if restored and sustained, would invigorate the future of our movement.

---

[5] Everett Ferguson, *The Early Church and Today*, volume 2 (Christian Life, Scripture, and Restoration), Abilene Christian University Press, 2014.

The next chapter begins a tour of some of our more notable doctrines described by Ferguson in the first chapter as the ecumenical non-distinctives of our movement. Grant Sullivan, another minister, pens chapter five concerning the role of baptism in our churches. Scott Elliott follows with a chapter on communion, a weekly rite of most Churches of Christ. My own contribution comes in chapter seven with a discussion of the fraying and controversial commitment of the Church of Christ to a cappella singing in our worship. In each chapter, the author will claim that while our rhetoric on these topics is often flawed, our commitment to the practice of each is commendable. These staples of our congregational identity are worth keeping, though often in need of reform.

Chapter eight follows this discussion of our common features by reminding us of how open the churches of Christ have been in the past. John Mark Hicks offers his own insight into our restoration heritage by exploring the "wild democracy" we have surrounding such issues as rebaptism, gender roles, and the Holy Spirit. Hicks argues in favor of the continuance of this heritage, united not by power structures but by vigorous debate.

Chapters nine, ten, and eleven are more personal in nature. Chris Altrock in artful fashion writes about the participation of the churches of Christ in his own life, acting as a matchmaker drawing him ever onward toward the marriage feast of the lamb. Professors Ron Highfield and John Wilson reflect on a lifetime in Churches of Christ and remind us of the virtue of blooming where we are planted. They offer a litany of simple graces evidenced in our congregations which are sometimes overlooked by the attention given to our faults.

Like canon itself, our compilation ends with an apocalypse, a parable in the mode of a ghost story. Theological librarian, Chris Rosser, gives us a tale of portraits and poetry aimed not so much at articulating a cerebral case but rather an artful call to the restoration heritage of self-criticism. To be a member of the Church of Christ is to be a critic of the Church of Christ.

So, what do we hope to accomplish here? Hope is certainly the right word in that question. We are hopeful that between naiveté and despair dwells hopeful honesty about who we are as a people. We hope that the frustrated will find again the optimism and virtue that should characterize our churches. We hope that the stagnant will notice that much work remains to be done in the unfinished task of restoration and reformation. We hope that the tide of talented ministers and members leaving our churches will be reversed. We hope that the kingdom of our Lord dwells in the Church of Christ for many years to come.

Benjamin J. Williams
Pulpit Mininster
Glenpool Church of Christ
Glenpool, Oklahoma

I Stayed for the Restoration Plea[1]

Everett Ferguson[2]

There is considerable uncertainty whether the traditional restoration approach is viable in these times. The validity of the restoration concept is the crucial question of the raison d'être of churches of Christ. Perhaps we as a people are not ready to undertake an inquiry concerning our fundamental assumptions, but it seems to me vitally important in these days to explore our foundation and determine what is built on rock and what is built on sand. This article offers the writer's understanding of what is valid restoration and some considerations in support of this approach. This is a preliminary enterprise designed to elicit discussion, and the writer welcomes replies.

Alexander Campbell and his associates spoke of their movement as "the current reformation." Later the terminology of "restoration" was developed in order to emphasize the need for a radical approach to remedying the ills of Christendom: not just a reformation of existing churches but a thorough going return to the faith and practice of the New Testament church.

---

[1] Originally printed as "The Validity of the Restoration Principle," *Mission* (August, 1973), 5–10. Used here with the permission of the author.

[2] Everett Ferguson is professor of church history emeritus at Abilene Christian University. Past president of the North American Patristics Society, Ferguson has been coeditor or editor of the *Journal of Early Christian Studies*, *Backgrounds of Early Christianity* (2003), *Recent Studies in Early Christianity* (1999), and *Encyclopedia of Early Christianity* (1990). He is author of *The Church of Christ: A Biblical Ecclesiology for Today* (1997).

Confusing Term

The word "restoration" in the sense in which it is ordinarily employed is not really a biblical word, and its meaning unfortunately is not always immediately obvious. At least it sometimes does not communicate too well. "Restoration" to an inhabitant of the British Isles means the "Restoration of the Monarchy" after the Cromwellian Commonwealth in the seventeenth century. A Harvard professor responded to the attempt of some students to explain their Restoration heritage with the comment, "Oh, so you want to be first-century Semites!" And then there was the Lutheran teacher of Church history who, after hearing me mention the *Restoration Quarterly*, referred to my connection with a renewal journal.

It is not evident that every current attempt to present the restoration plea gives attention to what was at the heart of the original movement to restore New Testament Christianity. A defense of the restoration plea, therefore, calls for some clarification as to what is meant by that plea. My reading from leaders in what is called "The Restoration Movement" has identified three significant emphases. I should like to propose what I consider to be the proper intention of each of these points.

The Biblical Ideal

To be the New Testament church today. This point will require further discussion, but immediately a negative clarification may be made. The earliest proponents did not understand the goal of restoring the New Testament church in a historical sense. The church in the first century had as many problems as anybody—false teaching, personal rivalries and misunderstandings, division. No one—not even contemporary charismatics, I presume—wants to restore exactly the church at Corinth. The plea to be the New Testament church today meant to take the apostolic teaching about the church as found in the New Testament as a guide and model. This apostolic teaching is wrapped up in history and cannot be separated from it. The biblical message was always spoken into a historical situation to meet a human need and not into a vacuum. It is thus difficult to sift the eternal from the temporal, and the historical setting participates in the revelation. Indeed there are many features in the actual first-century churches which are commendable, but this is not for their own sake but insofar as they reflect apostolic instructions. Determining those instructions is what must be accomplished in order to proceed to be the apostolic church in another time. It may be true that, as someone has observed, taking the New Testament teaching seriously will mean restoring some of the problems of the New Testament church as well. That would not, of course, be for their own sake, but as a by-product of trying to follow the apostles' teaching. At any rate, the appeal was to the biblical ideal rather than to the first-century church as it actually was with all its marks of imperfection involved in historical existence.

Neither Union Nor Uniformity

To practice the undenominational unity of the church. This unity was understood as neither union nor uniformity. Union would be a federation in which there is an agreement to disagree. Uniformity would be an agreement in opinions and all details. The unity envisioned was to be a solidarity in fellowship, an organic brotherhood. It was to be not just any kind of unity, but unity in Christ, yet a refusal to recognize the present denominational divisions as the proper condition of the church. Failure to achieve this unity has been one of the principal criticisms of the Restoration Movement. Without entering into a major response at this point, I may observe that failure to implement an ideal does not invalidate that ideal— the purpose of an ideal is to hold out a goal that has not been grasped. Imperfections in the implementation of the program of restoration may say more about human weakness and sinfulness than about something basically erroneous in the program itself. Even if not, the way the program has been attempted may be at fault rather than the concept of unity by restoration.

Restoring Humanity

To restore human beings to the image of God. Alexander Campbell saw this as the aim of the plea and the grand design of the Christian system. Restoration was not the goal but the means to the goal.

The ultimate goal was the restoration of humanity to fellowship with God. Restoration, therefore, involved more than just forms, institutions, externals. These things had their place, and in their place were important, but had to be kept in perspective. They served a larger design and purpose. Persons must be redeemed; they must be brought into a right relationship with God. One was to mature spiritually for eternal fellowship with God. Unless these things were achieved, all else was in vain.

Point one is the most controversial of the three. It is here that many of those who have been part of the Restoration heritage have concluded that modern historical, biblical, and theological studies have invalidated the restoration approach. Lessing's "ugly ditch" ("accidental truths of history can never become the proof of necessary truths of reason") has been cogently presented by F. G. Downing in his book *The Church and Jesus* (Studies in Biblical Theology Second Series, 10). If we understand the restoration of the New Testament church in the way suggested above, we may bypass many of the problems of historicity raised by Downing. That is, the restoration plea properly understood means to take the canon (as enshrining apostolic teaching and authority) as authority; it takes not the churches described but the church revealed in the New Testament as the pattern for church life today. (There is the subsequent question of what kind of pattern the New Testament provides, but this must await another study—some unfortunately think "pattern authority" is being rejected when it is only their understanding of the kind of pattern that is being questioned.) One, of course, cannot remove the canon from history in such a way as to make it an abstract ideal. There was an interaction between history and the formation of those books into a canon. My other work has demonstrated that I take history seriously in the context of canon. History has had a great deal to do with what we have received as the Scriptures and provides the proper way to determine their meaning. Nonetheless, if we take the canon as our authority, our norm is now settled by determining historically what the "early church" was and what its members believed and practiced. The concern becomes rather the following: we in our history, which has its problems, struggle to be what the apostles tried to help the early churches in their history to be. History is important for this task, but it does not say the only or the determinative word.

The first century fell short of the apostolic standard. So will we, no doubt; but that is no excuse for ignoring or not trying to follow that standard. The question here is whether it is valid to make the effort. Is it legitimate to attempt to construct a church from the biblical materials alone? This is primarily a question of theology and not of history.

It may indeed be pointed out that the approach presented thus far is begging some other, very hard questions. So be it. The attempt here will be to justify the concerns of the Restoration Movement, given its premises of canon and authority. With the clarifications offered concerning what is meant by the restoration plea, some arguments in its defense will now be presented.

Restoration Is Reasonable

The idea of restoration is *reasonable*. It is a common-sense kind of approach which, as will be seen below, is by no means unique to a small group of men of the American frontier of the nineteenth century. The inherent reasonableness of the restoration approach may be illustrated from J. G. Machen's book *Christianity and Liberalism*. An early twentieth-century Presbyterian fighting against the liberalism of his day which advanced religious naturalism under the guise of Christianity, Machen made the following argument:

> Christianity is an historical phenomenon, like the Roman Empire, or the Kingdom of Prussia, or the United States of America. And as an historical phenomenon it must be investigated on the basis of historical evidence.
>
> Is it true, then, that Christianity is not a doctrine but a life? The question can be settled only by an examination of the beginnings of Christianity. Recognition of that fact does not involve any acceptance of Christian belief; it is merely a matter of common sense and common honesty. At the foundation of the life of every corporation is the incorporation paper, in which the objects of the corporation are set forth. Other objects may be vastly more desirable than those objects, but if the directors use the name and the resources of the corporation to pursue the other objects they are acting *ultra vires* of the

corporation. So it is with Christianity. It is perfectly conceivable that the originators of the Christian movement had no right to legislate for subsequent generations; but at any rate they did have an inalienable right to legislate for all generations that should choose to bear the name "Christian." It is conceivable that Christianity may now have to be abandoned, and another religion substituted for it; but at any rate the question what Christianity is can be determined only by an examination of the beginnings of Christianity.

The beginnings of Christianity constitute a fairly definite historical phenomenon...But if any one fact is clear, on the basis of this evidence, it is that the Christian movement at its inception was not just a way of life in the modern sense, but a way of life founded upon a message. It was based, not upon mere feeling, not upon a mere program of work, but upon an account of facts. In other words it was based upon doctrine. (20, 21)

Machen's argument included what I consider to be the valid appeal to early Christian history but which I have chosen not to defend at the moment. His illustration of incorporation papers exactly fits the appeal to the Bible as the charter of Christianity. Machen's argument does exemplify the reasonableness of the restoration plea and demonstrates that one does not have to come from a restoration heritage to think in such terms. A great part of the appeal of the Campbell-Stone movements was that their preachers offered a rational, practical, no foolishness approach to religious problems.

Revelatory Religion

The idea of restoration has a *theological* basis. It is inherent in Christianity as a historical religion and is grounded in the doctrine of revelation. There are various types of religion. There are nature religions, such as most primitive religions and the Canaanite religion of Old Testament times. In nature religions the recurring cycles of nature determine the outlook and the religious practices. There is a great concern with the natural processes which sustain and propagate life. Then there are culture religions such as the religions of classical Greece and Rome and modern Hinduism. In culture religions the ceremonies are tied to the civilization; the religion is shaped by the culture, and itself exemplifies the culture. There are philosophic religions, such as Buddhism. A philosophic religion is founded on some timeless, universal principle. Finally, there are historical religions, such as Judaism, Christianity and Islam. They are sometimes called prophetic religions, because they look back to a prophet-founder whose word of revelation is authoritative. The historical religions came into existence as a result of a significant historical event viewed as revelatory and creating a community: Israel's exodus from Egypt, Jesus' death and resurrection, Mohammed's call. In historical religions decisive events and prophetic messages have been written in authoritative books—the Old Testament, New Testament, or the Quran. The point is that in a historical religion something decisive happened in the past which is normative for that faith. Thus there is always a pull to the past, a looking back to the sources, a concern with the way things were at the beginning of the religion. Jews, Christians, and Muslims may get rather far away from their origins, but they never do so completely without severing their religious ties, and they always include in their numbers "Orthodox" advocates of the contemporary authority of their Scriptures. This goes with being the type of religion which they are. Thus in Christian history when in the later Middle Ages the church appeared to have become a "folk religion" or a culture religion, the Renaissance arose with its slogan of "back to the sources."

A doctrine of revelation also accords with the "restoration" mentality. If God has spoken to human beings, this is religious authority for them. There is inherent in the idea of an authoritative revelation from God a concern for the sources. The nature, extent, and application of that authority are legitimate points for consideration. But the very reason they are is the premise that revelation occurred. The restoration plea is grounded theologically in the doctrine of revelation. Whether its advocates have always understood the revelation properly is another question, but the plea arises whenever the concept of revelation is present. I would ascribe primary importance to this theological argument for the idea of restoration.

Historical Expressions

The restoration idea has *historical* justification or support. The restoration or restitution of the New Testament church has been a recurring motif in church history. A. T. DeGroot assembled an astonishing number of religious groups having a wide variety of types of restoration emphasis in his book *The Restoration Principle*. Donald Durnbaugh's better focused study, *The Believer's Church*, has identified a particular church traced in later medieval movements, the Anabaptists, Puritans, Pietists, and Restorationists. Common emphases include, besides the motif of restitution, believers' membership, separation from the world, discipline, the Great Commission, religious liberty, and mutual aid. The restoration theme can be traced earlier in Christian history, as for example in monasticism. One does not have to make the claims of Broadbent's *The Pilgrim Church* to assert that a certain understanding of the nature of the church, its organization, its style of life, and its worship very similar to the Campbell-Stone movements have been recurring features of Christian history. There seems indeed to be something about the nature of Christianity that nurtures the restitution motif among its adherents and something about the nature of the biblical record that produces churches of the same general type when the effort is made to take it as normative for church life. This is not to say that these movements have agreed on all major points with the Campbells or that there is some sort of apostolic succession of dissent in Christian history. But it does say that the idea of restoration is not peculiar or unique. Its validity would be under considerable suspicion to my mind if it were. As the facts stand, restoration answers to a recurring urge, I would say an urge inherent in the nature of the Christian revelation.

Contemporary Interest

The idea of restoration has a *contemporary* interest. Modern biblical theology has shown a renewed respect for the biblical message and has opened up new insights into the meaning of that message. This concern for the meaning of the text is often accompanied by a lack of sympathy or even scorn for a "restoration" position, but many frankly look to the text for theological insights. Impatience with the limitations and failures of those who have championed restoration should not lead to a disregard for the biblical message at this time when respect for it is growing. Not only is contemporary biblical theology more favorable to the restoration position than the theologies current a few years ago, but there is interest in biblical renewal in old-line Protestant denominations, a massive awakening of biblical studies within Roman Catholicism and new youth movements which in their biblical literalism should convince even the most narrow restorationist that his movement is not really a part of fundamentalism. To be relevant is not to be right. But it would be surpassingly strange for members of a movement which has stressed biblical authority to depart from their restoration moorings just when the climate offers greater receptivity for this kind of message than has been available for a number of years.

Practical Implementation

The idea of restoration is *practical*. The preceding points have argued for the general validity of the principle of restoration. There are two further points which I would make on behalf of the particular expression of restorationism to be found among the churches of Christ. This plea has been found capable of practical application all over the world. It has been implemented independently by people around the world without knowledge of the American Restoration Movement. Both isolated individuals and whole groups have been involved. They have not come to conclusions on the peculiarities that have conditioned the American historical development – for instance, they have not had controversies over Bible classes or methods of cooperation—but on the nature of biblical message, human response to it, how to organize the church, and how to worship there has been a basic similarity. By way of contrast, no one has ever adopted Lutheran theology, to take one example out of many, without reading Luther's books or being taught by a Lutheran missionary. Yet many have taken only the New Testament and reached a common understanding of what it teaches. The *20th Century Christian* had a special issue, January, 1966, on some of these cases. That was not complete, but even the cases described there are an impressive demonstration of the practicality of taking the New Testament alone as a guide in church life.

Ecumenical

The restoration plea occupies ecumenical ground. Sometimes the plea has been presented in terms of distinction from others. Not so with the early advocates. It was presented as a uniting concept. And so it can be. The Churches of the restoration in their basic positions stand on the undivided ground of historic Christianity. Even the "distinctives" that are most characteristic of the movement are not really distinctive. Take the practice of immersion – virtually all Christians agree that immersion is valid baptism; none regard it as wrong. The position of those who practice sprinkling or pouring water is equally acceptable for valid baptism. But immersion is not a divisive concept; it is the only action that everyone agrees is acceptable. Or, consider vocal music in worship. No one has said a cappella singing is wrong; the contention is that instrumental music may acceptably be added. The common ground, universally accepted, is vocal music. The weekly communion is not considered wrong in Christendom. Many religious leaders (Calvin to name one) favored it but were not able to secure its practice. It is once more ecumenical ground in contrast to other practices (daily, monthly, quarterly, annually) which are not universally acceptable. Instead of stressing such practices as divisive, the "distinctives" are more properly uniting concepts. This approach is not an argument for what is right (which can be decided neither by the majority nor by a least common denominator), nor is it applicable to issues invented in modern times and not part of the historic practices of Christendom. But this approach is of importance for how one's position is presented.

These considerations argue for the validity of the general restoration approach. They are not all equally cogent, and their own validity will be differently assessed by different readers. The writer expects to learn from his readers.

I Stayed for the Love of Scripture

Jeremie Beller[1]

If there is one thing churches of Christ have been persistent about, it is our strong commitment to scripture. This commitment has been embedded in our spiritual DNA since the earliest days of the restoration movement. Even in the splintered state of churches of Christ today, traces of this gene remain present in virtually every segment.

Because I grew up in the churches of Christ, scripture has defined both my faith and family. *Give me the Bible* and *Holy Bible Book Divine* take me back to my childhood congregation where my grandfather served as an elder, my mother was my Bible class teacher, and my father was song leader, Bible class teacher, and occasional preacher. "All Scripture is given by the inspiration of God" was the first memory verse to earn me a star on the classroom chart. I was older than I would like to admit before realizing, "Speak where the Bible speaks" was not itself part of scripture. At age 15 I preached my first sermon (to use the term very loosely)

---

[1] Jeremie Beller has served as Congregational Minister for the Wilshire Church of Christ in Oklahoma City, Oklahoma, since 2002. He completed an MDiv from Oklahoma Christian University, and a PhD in Communication/Social Influence from the University of Oklahoma with a research focus on Religion and Racism. Along with his fulltime ministry responsibilities, Jeremie serves as an adjunct professor for Oklahoma Christian University. Jeremie and his wife, Delaina, have two children: Keaton and Kayden.

and was able to quote more texts-per-minute than the fastest member could locate.

Our fierce insistence on "book, chapter, and verse" explained our oddities to religious neighbors and friends. We used words differently than they did. In an effort to "call Bible things by Bible names," we seldom spoke of the "trinity," preferring the term "godhead" instead since it was in our KJVs. "Pastors" were elders, and every member a minister. Our rejection of instrumental music and infant baptism was our effort to be "silent where the Bible is silent." And every Christmas and Easter we reminded friends that scripture said nothing of either, nor does it say there were three wise men at the manger! We believed all religious division would disappear if only people would reject their religious traditions and return to the simplicity of scripture. It is, rather ironically, a tradition we have inherited from those before us.

Since the earliest days of the Restoration movement, the centrality of scripture and the plea to go back to the Bible have defined churches of Christ. As Barton W. Stone sought ordination into the Transylvania Presbytery of Kentucky, he was asked his willingness to adopt the Westminster Confession of Faith. Stone's answer became indicative of his future efforts: "I do, as far as I see it consistent with the word of God."[2] The same mindset eventually lead Stone and others to disband the Springfield Presbytery since scripture said nothing about such institutions. When the members of the Presbytery explained their decision, they made a definitive plea:

> We will, that the people henceforth take the Bible as the only sure guide to heaven; and as many as are offended with other books, which stand in competition with it, may cast them into the fire if they choose; for it is better to enter into life having one book, than having many to be cast into hell.[3]

Two years later, out of frustration with sectarian divisions across the American Frontier, Thomas Campbell determined to center his ministry on, "a plea for unity of all Christians upon the Bible

---

[2] Leroy Garrett, *The Stone-Campbell Movement: The Story of the American Restoration Movement* (Joplin: College Press, 2002), 98.

[3] For the text of "The Last Will and Testament of the Springfield Presbytery", see Charles A. Young, *Historical Documents Advocating Christian Union* (Chicago: Christian Century Company, 1904), pp 19-26.

alone."⁴ Campbell's efforts were summed up in the familiar motto that has defined generations of people who share his passion for restoration, "Where the Scriptures speak, we speak, and where the Scriptures are silent, we are silent." In what Leroy Garrett labeled "the founding document of the Stone-Campbell movement,"⁵ Campbell's *Declaration and Address* placed scripture squarely at in the heart of his work of restoration. To Campbell, "The New Testament is as perfect a constitution for the worship, discipline, and government of the New Testament church...as the Old Testament was for the...Old Testament church."⁶

This singular appeal to scripture was both a principled and practical stand for restoration leaders. They believed scripture was the revealed word of God for the church and it made little sense to set it aside for anything less. Campbell and others also grew disheartened with the seemingly arbitrary and political workings of denominational structure and traditions. The refusal to allow communion or fellowship based on denominational rules and regulations fueled the spirit of division. If unity were ever to come about, they would have to first rid themselves of that which caused the division. A simple appeal to scripture wrestled authority out of the hands of religious leaders and gave voice to anyone with a Bible. In the midst of the democratic mood taking root in America, this emphasis on the priesthood of all believers was an appealing proposition.⁷

We must be honest, however, and admit that this view of scripture is not unique to churches of Christ or the restoration movement. Long before Barton Stone or Thomas Campbell, others were making similar appeals. Reformation leaders challenged the authority of the Pope and the Catholic Church in large part through an appeal to *sola scriptura* (scripture alone). Though the concept would be interpreted in different ways, Luther, Zwingli, and Calvin appealed to the voice of scripture above all else. The

---

⁴ Garrett, 103.

⁵ Ibid., 94.

⁶ For the text of "Declaration and Address," see Young, *Historical Documents Advocating Christian Union*, pp. 27-209.

⁷ Nathan O. Hatch. *The Democratization of American Christianity*. (New Haven: Yale University Press, 1989).

translation and preservation of scripture done by Wycliffe, Tyndale, and others, often at the expense of their own lives, sprang from a commitment to the essential place of scripture and the desire to make it accessible to the common person. Even before arriving in America, Alexander Campbell was highly influenced by John Glas and other voices arguing strongly for a return to the New Testament. We were neither the first nor the only ones to appeal to the authority of scripture.

The centrality of scripture remains one of the most defining elements of churches of Christ. This seemingly simple appeal has been deemed "the genius of this movement"[8] and has served as the foundation for who we are and who we strive to be. Our view of scripture and the strong desire to align our life and doctrine with its contents remains our strength and provides us unique opportunities in the present religious climate.

The Case for Scripture

Christian faith is premised on the belief that without God we are nothing. By his power, we are created, and by his power, we are sustained. Because of our weakness and finiteness, salvation is initiated only as an act of God's grace. Any action of God for our benefit arises solely from grace. This includes scripture.

We can only speak of God because he has made himself known. Creation itself speaks to the majesty of God, displaying his power and care over creation (Ps. 19). Paul believed that certain "invisible attributes" of God were made known through creation (Rom. 1:20). The grandeur and reliability of creation reflect the majesty of its creator. Even today, scientists peering through microscopes or astronomers looking through telescopes catch glimpses of the majesty of God.

But certain aspects of God require special revelation if we are to discern his will for us. What is God's name? What does he desire from creation? How should we respond to him? These questions are not captured in the clouds; they require something more. For God to communicate directly to his creation in any form is an act of God reaching down to meet us. Because of our inability to grasp

---

[8] C. Leonard Allen and Richard T. Hughes, *Discovering Our Roots: the Ancestry of Churches of Christ* (Abilene: ACU Press, 1988), 3.

God on our own, we are dependent on his self-revelation. Jeremiah said: "Lord, I know that people's lives are not their own; it is not for them to direct their steps" (Jer. 10:23). Our only hope of knowing God is for God to make himself known.

Israel's claim to be a chosen people was built upon the assertion that God revealed himself to the nation in a special way. Because of this revelation, obedience to the covenant was possible, and none could claim the commandments of God were "too far away" (Deut. 30:12). Isaiah reminded the exiles that the ways and thoughts of God were higher than their own (Isa. 55:5-11). Citing words from Isaiah, Paul contrasts the wisdom of the cross with the wisdom of the world, asking, "For who has known the mind of the Lord so as to instruct him?" (1 Cor. 2:16; Isa. 40:13).

Sometimes God reveals himself through an event in history, later to be confirmed within the community and recorded in scripture. Any time new revelation is claimed, this pattern emerges. The call of Moses first appears as a private endeavor. Sitting alone on a mountain watching his father-in-law's sheep, Moses claimed an encounter with God (Exod 4). Moses' words were later confirmed through the actions of God and witnessed by the wider community. Through the plagues, crossing of the sea, and eventual experiences at Sinai, the community personally encountered God in a way that verified Moses' assertion. What Moses claimed to receive on the Mountain—both at his initial calling and the reception of the law—is confirmed to the broader community through these events.

A similar pattern unfolds with New Testament scripture. Jesus claimed his life and ministry were the ultimate fulfillment of Old Testament scripture (Matt. 5:17). His announcement that "the Kingdom of Heaven is near" (Matt. 4:17) was verified publically by appealing to accepted scripture, healings, and his eventual resurrection. Because the church accepted the validity of Jesus' claims—and believers would argue the Holy Spirit moved them—New Testament authors recorded the stories, which the church regarded inspired and authoritative in their retelling.

God also reveals himself through the process of writing. The tablets which Moses carried off the mountain were God's revelation to Israel (Exod. 34:4). They were more than simply the historical record of what had taken place on the mountain; they were themselves God's revelation. In the same way, Paul's letters were God's revelation in their writing (1 Cor. 14:37).[9]

Jews and Christians viewed the events, their retelling in scripture, and the writings themselves all as a revelation of God (2 Tim. 3:16 and 2 Pet. 1:20). The authority of past events continued in their telling and retelling. The authority of written words was captured in their very origin. God is believed to be at work in scripture within the historical account and as an ongoing expression. As NT Wright notes:

> The apostolic writings, like the 'word' which they now wrote down, were not simply about the coming of God's Kingdom into the world; they were, and were designed to be, part of the means whereby that happened, and whereby those through whom it happened could themselves be transformed into Christ's likeness.[10]

At its most basic level, the crafting and acceptance of scripture represent an insight into the stories that defined the earliest Christians as well as the doctrines and practices they followed. Scripture was their understanding of Jesus and the faith proclaimed by the apostles. From a purely historical perspective, scripture benefits from its proximity to the life of the early church. If viewed through the lens of inspiration, the testimony of scripture gains significantly more weight than a mere historical record.

Even as the early church accepted the ongoing work of revelation through the power of the Holy Spirit, scripture was viewed as an authoritative companion and measure of God's continuing revelation. Luke's Gospel begins with the reassurance that the things handed down had been carefully investigated and declared a fulfillment of scripture (Luke 1:1-3). Peter's claim to speak by the power of the Spirit is confirmed with a recitation of Joel (Acts 2:16). Even Luke's picture of Paul as a transformed and God-sent messenger is subjected to verification of scripture (Acts 17:11). In his own letters, Paul believed that he spoke the words of God (1 Cor. 14:37)

---

[9] Whether the New Testament authors understood they were writing scripture is beyond the point. The inclusion of these letters in the canon indicates the Church viewed them as revelatory in their writing.

[10] N.T. Wright, *The Last Word: Beyond the Bible Wars to a New Understanding of the Authority of Scripture*, (New York: Harper One, 2005), 51.

but still worked to demonstrate their continuity with scripture (Rom. 15:4). As impressive as any "eyewitness to the majesty of Jesus" may be (2 Pet. 1:16), 2 Peter still argues that the message of scripture was more than a private human endeavor; it was a revealing act of God through the Holy Spirit (2 Pet. 1:19-21). Claims of new revelation were subjected to the test of consistency with accepted scripture.

Any assertion of religious authority outside of scripture raises fundamental questions of credibility. What confidence can we place in religious leaders if their message is inconsistent with the story and teachings of scripture? What standard could be used to discern claims of new revelation that contradict or amend what is revealed in scripture? If ecclesiastical tradition and authority are given precedent over scriptural authority, how do we recognize the proper ecclesiastical body or by what standard is such a body held to account? If that ecclesiastical body loses its way, how does it find its way back?

If the same Spirit of God guides individuals and ecclesiastical bodies that inspired apostles and prophets to pen scripture, we should expect consistency among them. If not, then either God's credibility is in question, or far more likely, someone else's credibility is at risk. To substantiate authoritative claims, one must do so through either blind faith, unsubstantiated tradition, or eventually, some regard to scripture.

If scripture is viewed as the revealed will of God, those who seek God cannot ignore it. Any efforts at restoration can only take place when we do our best to conform our lives and doctrine to what God has made known. Allen, Hughes, and Weed are correct:

> We must see more clearly that Scripture is not so much an ancient text that we can master with carefully refined study techniques as it is an ancient text through which God seeks to master us. We must read it submissively, in the frailty of mind and body, and thereby experience again and again the life-giving and transforming power of God.[11]

As we conform to his will, restoration will follow. After 57 years of neglecting the will of God, King Josiah led Judah in a restoration

---

[11] Allen, Hughes, and Weed, 71.

sparked in part by the discovery of "the book of the Law"(2 Kings 22-23). Ezra and Nehemiah's spiritual renewal culminated in a public reading from the book of the Law (Neh. 9:3). Restoration takes place only when God's people conform their lives to the revealed will of God.

Legitimate Concerns

A strong commitment to scripture is obviously not without objection. Attacks and concerns have been expressed by forces both inside and outside of Christian faith. Voices in popular media wonder why 21st-century people would cling to a 1st-century book written in a different language and to a different people. Admittedly, the concept seems old-fashioned and out of touch to nonbelievers and even some believers who view a close commitment to scripture as little more than, "the bondage of spiritual captivity of dead men".[12] At first glance, scripture appears silent to some of the most pressing issues of our day. Even when it does share modern concerns, it does so with a pre-modern view of the world. Seeking relevance, it is tempting to dispense with scriptural perspectives and replace them with the more up-to-date, accepted perspectives.

If scripture were nothing more than a cold record of historical facts and figures, these critics would have a valid point. If, however, scripture is truly "God-breathed" (2 Tim. 3:16), then it is more than the words of dead men. Those who reject the possibility of the Christian story naturally reject claims of inspiration since it lies outside the allowances of their worldview.

Accepting the story of scripture without accepting the authority of scripture is a difficult position to hold. Scripture's story points to Jesus as the ultimate act of God's revelation and the fulfillment of scripture. He is the one to whom scripture pointed (Luke 24:27). Claiming "all authority in heaven and on earth" (Matt. 28:18), Jesus did not dismiss scripture and replace it with something new; he amplified and embodied it. Scripture pointed to Jesus, and Jesus pointed to scripture. Those of us who accept Christian faith and the claim of scripture's inspired nature can

---

[12] Alexander J. Barron, "Why the Bible Is Not the Word of God." *The Huffington Post.* Accessed March 14, 2016. www.huffingtonpost.com/alexander-j-barron/why-the-bible-is-not-the-_b_7717552.html.

hardly reject the implications. Believers and non-believers have their reasons for holding their positions, but if God has revealed himself through scripture, then it is a voice to which every culture should listen.

It is true that scripture does not explicitly speak to some modern concerns of science, ethics, culture, and politics. Even in its first-century setting, the New Testament left issues unnoted in name. Yet, the Bible does not intend itself to be a quick reference guide to every question encountered. Instead, it concerns itself with the story of God and his interaction with creation. It calls us to trust him and model our lives after his crucified son. Doing so will not always immediately indicate the clearest response to modern questions, but it will lay the foundation from which to guide our investigation. It is worth noting, however, that many of the biggest challenges of our day rest in the basic endeavor to obey the clearest call of scripture: "Love the Lord your God with all your heart and with all your soul and with all your strength and with all your mind" and "Love your neighbor as yourself" (Lk. 10:27). Mastery of these concerns will go far in the mastery of others.

Our commitment to scripture has also been challenged by calling into question the credibility of scripture's story. Modern scholars pose doubts whether a truly orthodox Christian faith ever existed and argue the New Testament perspective is simply the product of the winning side of a lengthy argument.[13] As complicated as canonization may be, some things remain certain. First, Christian faith has consistently grounded itself in what it believes to be historical events (life, death, and resurrection of Jesus). These events provide a fundamental orthodoxy from the earliest days of Christianity. Second, writings that were recognized as authoritative were viewed as such in part because of their consistency with accepted scripture and tradition. The teachings of Marcion and Gnostic teachers were considered contradictory to already accepted Old Testament scripture and apostolic tradition. What emerged as the

---

[13] Bart D. Ehrman, *Lost Christianities: The Battle for Scripture and the Faiths We Never Knew*, (New York: Oxford Press, 2003). See also Bart D. Ehrman, *Lost Scripture: Books that Did Not Make it into the New Testament*, (New York: Oxford Press, 2003).

accepted canon was anything but a random theological novelty. Finally, Wright makes an important observation concerning the early Christian views of scripture:

> We should note, as of some importance in the early history of the Bible-reading church, that those who were being burned alive, thrown to the lions, or otherwise persecuted, tortured and killed were normally those who were reading Matthew, Mark, Luke, John, Paul and the rest. The kind of spirituality generated by "Thomas" and similar books would not have worried the Roman imperial authorities, for reasons not unconnected with the fact that "Thomas" and the similar collection of sayings are non-narratival, deliberately avoiding the option of placing the sayings within the overarching framework of the story of Israel.[14]

Even within churches of Christ, worries that our high view of scripture tends toward bibliolatry have been expressed.[15] If scripture is viewed as an end in itself, the critique is warranted. Stripped of its connection to the authority of God and its purpose of creating faith, scripture becomes a lifeless list of pointless commands and ritual. Yet the very reason the church holds scripture in high regard is because it is viewed as a revelation *from* God and not just a revelation *about* God (2 Tim. 3:16; 2 Pet. 1:20; Heb. 4:12). Its purpose is to create faith in those who encounter it (John 20:31). As Achtemier put it: "It is, in the final analysis, not the text that matters, but the one to whom the text points." [16]

---

[14] Wright, 63-64. For an accessible reaction to Ehrman and similar claims, see Ben Witherington III, "Why the 'Lost Gospels' Lost Out,: *Christianity Today*, June 1, 2004. V 48. No 6.

[15] Christopher Hudson expressed this concern in his review of Kenneth L. Cukrowski, Mark W. Hamilton., and James W. Thompson, *God's Holy Fire: The Nature and Function of Scripture* (Abilene: ACU Press, 2002). He felt the authors' argument for the "infallibility" of scripture and their position that "if tradition conflicts with Scripture, we follow Scripture; if reason or experience conflicts with Scripture, we will follow Scripture" tended toward bibliolatry. See Christopher Hudson, review of *God's Holy Fire: The Nature and Function of Scripture*, by Kenneth L. Cukrowski, Mark W. Hamilton, and James W. Thompson, *Restoration Quarterly* 44 (2002): 117-19.

[16] Paul J. Achtemeier, *Inspiration and Authority: Nature and Function of Christian Scripture* (Peabody: Hendrickson, 1999), 146

It may be that frustration with our view of scripture is a reaction to the unmet expectations of restoration leaders. Stone, Campbell, and others believed that if people only left behind denominational creeds and councils and accepted the simplicity of scripture, then unity would ultimately prevail. Sadly, disunity continues in abundance. "Speak where the Bible speaks and be silent where the Bible is silent" is great in principle but challenging in practice. Well-intentioned and well-educated people struggle to explain how it is that scripture speaks and what it means when scripture is silent. As a result, churches who share a strong commitment to scripture and a passion for restoration are too often divided even among themselves.[17]

The problem, however, does not rest in scripture, but in those who handle it. An authoritative view of scripture does not equate to an authoritative view of the interpreter, nor the interpretive method used. When his opponents used scripture to condemn him, Jesus placed the fault on the readers and not scripture (John 5:29; Matt. 22:29). Knowing Paul's writings and other scripture had already been twisted, the author of 2 Peter continued to pen what would eventually be accepted as more scripture (2 Pet. 3:16). Scripture cannot be held accountable for its misreading or misapplication by its readers any more than Jesus should be held accountable for those who reject him. To borrow from Paul, "let God be true, but every man a liar" (Rom. 3:4, NIV).

Going Forward

Our commitment to scripture provides tremendous opportunity in the current religious climate. Scripture provides a stable ground in

---

[17] This challenge is seen in the debate over the role of women in the church. Matthew Morine, "The Feminist Agenda in Churches of Christ." *Gospel Advocate*, September 2015, suggests that those holding an egalitarian view of women's roles reject "the plain teaching of the Word of God" and hold a "disregard for the intent of scripture." Mike Cope responded by noting, "What's different isn't commitment to scripture or willingness to study scripture but conclusions about scripture." See Mike Cope, "Judgment-Free Disagreements: A Response to Matthew Morine." PreacherMike RSS. Accessed March 15, 2016. http://preachermike.com/2015/10/08/judgment-free-disagreements-a-response-to-matthew-morine.

the midst of the upheaval encountered by each generation. Scripture links our story with the story of God's people in the past and gives direction to the unfolding story of his Kingdom. It reminds us that we stand in line with women and men of faith who, in their own weakness, sought God and nurtured their faith through the same stories, words, and actions. Scripture provides meaning that transcends present and passing fads while calling us back to a faith greater than ourselves.

Our strong commitment to scripture also comes with challenges. It forces us to be honest with our own traditions. Restoration leaders viewed tradition as one of the culprits of division and believed scripture demanded its abandonment. Tradition, however, sneaks up on us when we least expect it: when we interpret scripture, when we immerse people into Christ, when we meet on Sunday nights or ask God to "guard, guide and direct us." These are all traditions, but not all traditions are created equally. Jesus condemned some traditions (Matt. 15:6) whereas Paul called the church to be faithful to tradition (2 Thess. 2:15).[18]

The problem is we use the same word to describe different things. Some traditions are "biblical" in their expression of a direct and clear response to scripture. We practice immersion because of biblical precedent and theology. Bible class, Sunday night meetings, and invitation songs, however, are principled traditions, grounded in a desire to express a principle found in scripture (fellowship, study, response) even while lacking clear biblical expression. Some traditions are just practical ways of doing things: what time we meet, the order of worship, where we meet. All three—biblical, principal, and practical—are traditions, but not of equal standing. To equate principled or practical tradition with Biblical tradition weakens our commitment to scripture, destroys our credibility, and makes us worthy of the same rebuke Jesus leveled at the Pharisees (Matt. 15:3).

We must also be cautious that our commitment to scripture does not become an arrogant rejection of legitimate voices only to be replaced by private interpretation or preference. The reading and interpretation of scripture are to be done within the community of believers and not as an individual license to twist scripture to our liking (2 Pet. 1:20). Accepting the authority of scripture is

---

[18] The word translated "tradition" in both texts is the same: παραδόσεις.

an acknowledgment of our inability to control or manipulate God. Proper reading and application of scripture begin with humility.

Finally, our devotion to scripture must be matched with a commitment to know and share the Jesus to whom it points. Parents should teach their children, and every believer should spend time in its pages to see Jesus. When the church gathers, it is the voice of God that needs to be heard above all else. Preaching and teaching should bring the words of scripture to life so that the church can hear God's voice and be shaped in the image of Christ. If we truly believe scripture is inspired, we will open its pages to breathe in the breath of God.

This deep commitment to scripture is one reason I have remained committed to churches of Christ. Despite the temptation to misuse scripture, efforts to conform our lives and doctrine to its message remain an enduring strength of churches of Christ. Without scripture, we are left vulnerable to the same challenges of human frailty and misconduct of any other approach, yet without an objective, measurable way back. Like the early church, claims to speak on God's behalf must be filtered through the test of existing scripture. Even though we may differ in how scripture speaks and what its silence means, scripture provides the foundation and framework upon which to focus our discussion and call us back to the will of God.

To be the church of Jesus Christ is to be a body of people longing to know God's will. By his grace, God reached down to make himself known. Driven by his desire for us to live in his presence, he revealed himself through scripture. In its Old Testament form scripture prepared people to see Jesus. In its New Testament form, it points us back to his story and helps prepare us to see him again.

Bibliography

Allen, Crawford Leonard., and Richard T. Hughes. *Discovering Our Roots: The Ancestry of Churches of Christ*. Abilene, TX: ACU Press, 1988.

Barron, Alexander J. "Why the Bible Is Not the Word of God." The Huffington Post. Accessed March 14, 2016. http://www.huffingtonpost.com/alexander-j-barron/why-the-bible-is-not-the-_b_7717552.html.

Cope, Mike. "Judgment-Free Disagreements: A Response to Matthew Morine." PreacherMike (blog), October 2015. Accessed March 15, 2015. http://preachermike.com/.

Cukrowski, Kenneth L., Mark W. Hamilton, and James Thompson. *God's Holy Fire: The Nature and Function of Scripture*. Abilene, TX: ACU Press, 2002.

Ehrman, Bart D. *Lost Christianities: The Battle for Scripture and the Faiths We Never Knew*. New York: Oxford University Press, 2003.

Ehrman, Bart D. *Lost Scriptures: Books That Did Not Make It into the New Testament*. New York: Oxford University Press, 2003.

Garrett, Leroy. *The Stone-Campbell Movement: The Story of the American Restoration Movement*. Joplin, MO: College Press, 1994.

Hatch, Nathan O. *The Democratization of American Christianity*. New Haven: Yale University Press, 1989.

Hudson, Christopher. "Review of God's Holy Fire: The Nature and Function of Scripture" by Kenneth L. Cukrowski, Mark W. Hamilton, and James W. Thompson. *Restoration Quarterly* 44 (2002): 117-19

Morine, Matthew. "The Feminist Agenda in Churches of Christ." *Gospel Advocate*, September 2015.

Witherington, Ben. "Why the 'Lost Gospels' Lost Out." *Christianity Today*, June 1, 2004.

Wright, N. T. *The Last Word: Beyond the Bible Wars to a New Understanding of the Authority of Scripture*. San Francisco: Harper, 2005.

Young, Charles A. *Historical Documents, Advocating Christian Union: Epochmaking Statements by Leaders among the Disciples of Christ for the Restoration of the Christianity of the New Testament—Its Doctrines, Its Ordinances, and Its Fruits*. Chicago: The Christian Century Company, 1904.

I Stayed for the Christ in the Church of Christ

Matthew Dowling[1]

Today, close observers of the Churches of Christ will have a hard time discerning what it is that holds us together doctrinally or theologically. Among those who know me, my oft-heard quip that we are living in doctrinal days akin to the Wild West will soon be tested for its truthfulness. Perhaps this is not surprising; after all, the Churches of Christ have a bit of everything in us – some of the five points of Calvinism but lots more of Arminian Remonstrant theology, a dash of the amillenial or dispensationalist but more often a wonderful myriad of eschatological viewpoints, a polity shaped by our Presbyterian and Baptist forefathers but a dedication to autonomous congregational identity, and a commitment to radical primitivism but a concern among some to identify as *the* New Testament church. In addition to these things, one might observe still-marginalized but notable voices advocating for egalitarianism, open theism, Christian universalism, private inclusivism,

---

[1] Matthew Dowling has served as the preaching minister at the Plymouth Church of Christ since 2016. He holds degrees in science and theology and is currently a ThM student in Historical Theology at Puritan Reformed Theological Seminary. Matthew has served churches of Christ in Oklahoma, New Jersey, and Michigan. Matthew and Rachel have 4 children: Gabriel, Gideon, Trinity, and Abram. Matthew regularly blogs about matters pertaining to Christianity, the Church, and life in Christ at http://www.matthewdowling.org.

and a host of theological commitments not usually associated with the Churches of Christ. Some of us see ourselves as an ecumenical people; some of us see ourselves as a sectarian people, the true church. The ideological camps within our churches are often described as conservative or progressive-liberal. All of this and more shape us today. In the face of this diversity, the question remains: what is it that binds us together theologically? To be frank, I am concerned that more than ever we are a divided people because we can no longer articulate what precisely holds us together. We often can only articulate where we each sit on a spectrum of belief or thought in general.

As I survey the landscape of the churches of Christ from the perspective of a preaching minister, I am reminded of a problem Paul faced in Corinth, a situation of division and disunity. Typical for Paul, the solution to the problem in Corinth was to be found in the gospel of Jesus Christ and in correct thinking about ourselves, others, and the God who possesses us. He wrote,

> Let no man deceive himself. If any man among you thinks that he is wise in this age, let him become foolish that he may become wise. For the wisdom of this world is foolishness before God. For it is written, "He is the one who catches the wise in their craftiness"; and again, "The Lord knows the reasonings of the wise, that they are useless." So then let no one boast in men. For all things belong to you, whether Paul or Apollos or Cephas or the world or life or death or things present or things to come; all things belong to you, and you belong to Christ; and Christ belongs to God. (1 Cor. 3:18–23, NASB)

Much division in the church would be eliminated if individuals were not so impressed with their own wisdom. Unfortunately, many of the Corinthian converts carried their spirit of philosophical factionalism into the church (1 Cor. 1:18-25). We do the same today when as people on both sides of the spectrum in the Churches of Christ we divide according to our philosophical viewpoints. In this division, there is seemingly nothing to rally around. But the general intent of what Paul is saying to the philosophically oriented Corinthians can be stated like this to us today:

Since you have become Christians, have been filled by God's Spirit, and recognize the Scriptures as His Word, you have no more need for philosophy. It did not help you when you were unbelievers and it will certainly not help you now that you believe. Give it up. It has nothing to offer but confusion and division. You are now united around God's supreme revelation in Jesus Christ. Don't be misled and split by human speculations.

Proposal

Rather than remain split around human speculations, I want to propose an exercise—a kind of theological triage—one that has been the provenance and project for several years of Dr. Albert Mohler, president of Southern Baptist Theological Seminary.[2] I think it might prove useful for the Churches of Christ. Dr. Mohler writes,

> For some years now, I have been arguing for another conceptual model of understanding our theological responsibility and the task of defining which doctrines are central and essential to our faith. I discovered this model in a hospital emergency room, where medical personnel have to make decisions very similar to those we face in the theological task. Emergency medical personnel practice a discipline known as triage—a process that allows trained personnel to quickly evaluate relative medical urgency. Given the chaos of an emergency room reception area, someone must be armed with the medical expertise to make an immediate determination of medical priority. Which patients should be rushed into surgery? Which patients can wait for a less urgent examination? Medical personnel cannot flinch from asking these questions and taking responsibility to treat the patients with the most critical needs, since those patients are the top priority.

---

[2] Albert Mohler's initial piece on "theological triage" appeared in Daniel Akin's book *A Theology for the Church* (Nashville, Tennessee: B&H Publishing Group, 2007), 927-34. He has most recently written on this topic in the book *Four Views on the Spectrum of Evangelicalism (Grand Rapids, Michigan: Zondervan, 2011), 77-80.*

Mohler's proposal resonated with me. When I was in college, I worked in a local emergency room as a critical care technician, a kind of medically specialized orderly. It was in the ER that I learned the process called *triage*. The word triage comes from the French word *trier*, which means "to sort." Like Dr. Mohler, I believe the same discipline that brings order to the hectic arena of the emergency room might offer assistance to the Churches of Christ as we seek what it is that fundamentally "binds the center" of our doctrinal convictions. This proposal is meant to aid in the clarification of what is most important to us doctrinally, useful for elders, ministers, and lay leaders as a doctrinal exercise for the congregation. We have no ecclesial body, denominational committee, etc. that would institute or administer such a proposal, but it could be useful within the context of the local church, which is the sphere of my greatest concern. With that caveat mentioned, Dr. Mohler's proposal is that we distinguish between three orders of doctrine:

1. First-Order Doctrines: issues of such importance that a denial of them would mean the eventual denial of Christianity itself.
2. Second-Order Doctrines: doctrines upon which Christians may disagree, but which may create significant boundaries between believers, whether as distinct congregations or between denominational fellowships.
3. Third-Order Doctrines: doctrines upon which Christians may disagree but yet remain in close fellowship, even within local congregations.

As is evident, this segregation of doctrines within three different orders is focused on *doctrinal* content for reasons that will be explained below. What is important to note is that if we are going to understand better what binds our theological center, we will need to be able to discern between doctrines that are absolutely central to our faith versus doctrines around which we have more liberty. In Dr. Mohler's proposal, a discipline of theological or doctrinal triage would require us to sort beliefs into three different levels of theological urgency, each corresponding to a set of issues and theological priorities found in current doctrinal debates.

But how do we do this? In addition to the Mohler proposal, a promising rubric for distinguishing where a doctrine might fall within these three orders (or some other doctrinal hierarchy) is one based on a proposal by Dr. Erik Thoennes, professor and department chair of biblical and theological studies at Biola University.[3] According to Dr. Thoennes' proposal, we weigh the cumulative force of at least seven considerations:

1. Relevance to the essence of the gospel;
2. Relevance to the character of God;
3. Biblical clarity;
4. Biblical frequency and significance (how often in Scripture it is taught, and what weight Scripture places upon it);
5. Effect on other doctrines;
6. Consensus among Christians (past and present); and
7. Effect on personal and church life.

These criteria for determining the importance of particular beliefs must be considered in light of their cumulative weight regarding the doctrine being considered. The ability to discern the relative importance of theological beliefs is vital for Christian life and ministry. All of Thoennes' considerations could be considered collectively in determining how important a doctrine is to the Christian faith (and used to place that doctrine in its 'order'). The ability to rightly discern the difference between core doctrines and legitimately disputable matters will keep the Churches of Christ from either compromising important truth or needlessly dividing over peripheral issues.

Living as we do in an age of widespread doctrinal denial and intense theological confusion, the Churches of Christ must rise to the challenge of communicating clearly our precious Christian

---

[3] Erik Thoennes, *Life's Biggest Questions: What the Bible Says about the Things That Matter Most* (Grand Rapids: Crossway, 2011), 35-37. Thoennes writes, "We should consider the cumulative weight of these criteria when determining the relative importance of particular beliefs. For instance, just the fact that a doctrine may go against the general consensus among believers (see item 6) does not necessarily mean it is wrong, although that might add some weight to the argument against it. All the categories should be considered collectively in determining how important an issue is to the Christian faith. The ability to rightly discern the difference between core doctrines and legitimately disputable matters will keep the church from either compromising important truth or needlessly dividing over peripheral issues" (36-37).

truth and inheritance. We must sort the issues with a trained mind and a humble heart, in order to protect what the Apostle Paul called the "treasure" that has been entrusted to us. Given the urgency of this challenge, a lesson from the emergency room just might help.

Why Doctrine Matters

Why the emphasis on doctrine in this proposal? Simply put, it is because doctrine is, quite literally, the teaching of the church–what the church understands to be the substance of its faith. "Great saints have always been dogmatic," says A. W Tozer.[4] J.I. Packer, the great Anglican theologian, reminds us "…there can be no spiritual health without doctrinal knowledge."[5] Troublingly, the past century witnessed an increasingly energetic revolt against doctrine. A denial of specific formulations of classical Christian doctrine has been evident in some quarters, while others have rejected the very notion of doctrine itself, particularly in the Churches of Christ.[6] This is surprising. While Christians have given clear witness to the necessity of personal faith in Jesus Christ, that personal faith is based on some specific understanding of who Jesus Christ is and what He accomplished on the cross. After all, we do not call persons to profess faith in faith, but faith in Christ. There is no Christianity "in general." Faith in some experience devoid of theological or biblical content, no matter how powerful, is not New Testament Christianity. Those called to Christianity may believe nothing in particular. But to be frank: *faith resides in particulars*. No more than a

---

[4] A. W. Tozer, *A Treasury of A. W. Tozer* (Grand Rapids: Baker Book House, 1980), 174.

[5] J. I. Packer, *Knowing God* (Downers Grove, IL: InterVarsity Press, 1973), 17.

[6] Olbricht makes such a note on the state of doctrine in his entry for 'theology' in the Churches of Christ in the *Stone-Campbell Encyclopedia*. Of course, doctrinal or theological formulation has regularly enjoyed hard times among the Churches of Christ because of the contention that we simply follow the Bible. But what I mean by doctrine is systematic biblical teaching on topics like God, Jesus Christ, the Holy Spirit, revelation, faith, humanity, sin, salvation, creation, the church, sanctification, and eschatology. Surely the Bible has much to say about these doctrinal and theological loci.

patient should be content with a cardiologist who exhibits a comforting bedside manner and yet is ignorant of the circulatory system should congregants settle for zeal without knowledge.[7]

Those who sow disdain and disinterest in biblical doctrine will reap a harvest of rootless and fruitless Christians. Ample evidence of this neglect is readily apparent. In this respect, Paul's warning to his protégé Timothy is particularly timely, "the time will come when they will not endure sound doctrine" (2 Timothy 4:3). In our time, few tolerate doctrine at all. This intolerance accounts for the paradigm shifts we have seen in our own shift: from God to the self and from doctrine to the subjective usefulness of religion and spirituality for private well-being which is evident in both conservative and liberal circles.[8] In fact, sociologist Christian Smith has characterized this rootless, subjective spirituality as "Moralistic Therapeutic Deism."[9] Michael Horton warns of the root problem with pursuing a faith bent on experience but devoid of theological or doctrinal content:

> …if the truth or importance of doctrine is determined by what we consider most useful for our moral improvement and religious experience, many of the most important Christian doctrines will lose their weight and eventually their saliency. If we imagine that we already know what we need to believe, experience, and pursue, then the doctrine of the Trinity, for example, will seem practically irrelevant. Only by beginning with the Trinity, reevaluating every topic in systematic theology and

---

[7] Illustration from Michael Horton, *The Christian Faith: A Systematic Theology for Pilgrims on the Way* (Grand Rapids, MI: Zondervan, 2011), 97.

[8] Ibid., 99.

[9] Christian Smith and Melinda Lundquist Denton, *Soul Searching: The Religious and Spiritual Lives of American Teenagers* (New York: Oxford Univ. Press, 2005), 162. In terms of MTD, the authors found that many young people believed in several moral statutes not exclusive to any of the major world religions. It is this combination of beliefs that they label Moralistic Therapeutic Deism: 1) A god exists who created and ordered the world and watches over human life on earth; 2) God wants people to be good, nice, and fair to each other, as taught in the Bible and by most world religions; 3) The central goal of life is to be happy and to feel good about oneself; 4) God does not need to be particularly involved in one's life except when God is needed to resolve a problem; 5) Good people go to heaven when they die. These points of belief were compiled from interviews with approximately 3,000 teenagers.

church practice, and reimagining our lives as the result of the distinct yet undivided work of the Father, the Son, and the Spirit does the doctrine prove its own practical value. Furthermore, modern atheism's critique of religion as nothing more than the projection of human longings and felt needs becomes more persuasive if we restrict the object of theology to whatever we happen to find useful.[10]

What is important to remember is that from the earliest days of the church's history, Christians have made the journey from Scripture to doctrine, and isolating scriptural doctrine from Christian ministry cannot be sustained biblically. J. Gresham Machen labeled this kind of thinking "the modern hostility to doctrine."[11] D. Martyn Lloyd-Jones warned, "we cannot have the benefits of Christianity if we shed its doctrines."[12] Christianity resists being separated from doctrine because the Christian movement is a way of life rooted in revelation, a biblical message. That is reflected in Paul telling Timothy to watch both his life and his doctrine closely (1 Tim. 4:16). Biblically speaking, Christian doctrine is scriptural truth. Two New Testament words are most often translated doctrine, teaching, or instruction—*didachē* and *didaskalia*.[13] A comparison of their combined fifty-one appearances affirms that Christian doctrine refers to scripture, whether read, explained, or even theologically systematized. Perhaps the modern avoidance of doctrine lies partially in the fact that "doctrine" has been understood too narrowly like a doctrinal statement or theological essay, rather than more broadly in the scriptural sense of biblical content.[14]

No approach to doctrine, other than taking it seriously, makes sense out of Christ's command for the disciples to teach obedience to all that He commanded them (Matt 28:20). Or Paul's ministry to the Ephesian elders by proclaiming the whole will of God (Acts 20:27). Or the angel's command for the apostles to speak "the full

---

[10] Horton, *Christian Faith*, 99.

[11] J. Gresham Machen, *Christianity and Liberalism* (Grand Rapids: Eerdmans, 2009), 18

[12] D. Martyn Lloyd-Jones, *I Am Not Ashamed* (Grand Rapids: Baker Book House, 1986), 92.

[13] R. E. Nixon, "Doctrine," ed. D. R. W. Wood et al., *New Bible Dictionary* (Leicester, England; Downers Grove, IL: InterVarsity Press, 1996), 280.

[14] Ibid.

message of this new life" (Acts 5:20). Or Paul's mandate for Timothy to pass the apostolic teachings on to the next generation (2 Tim 2:2). Or Christ's commendation to the Ephesian church for taking doctrine seriously (Rev 2:2,6). This is why the proposal I am advocating is essentially *doctrinal* in nature.

There is a well-trodden line that gets wielded without discernment so often these days, "God doesn't care *what* you believe so long as you are *sincere*." It's a statement rooted in the kind of thinking which leads many to conclude that all religions lead ultimately to the same reality. As is often argued, it doesn't matter which road you take, so long as you follow your chosen path faithfully and *sincerely*. To such a notion, the Christian who accepts the Bible as the infallible and inerrant rule of faith and life, hears the voice of scripture speak, "There is a way which seems right to a man, but its end is the way of death" (Proverbs 14:12; 16:25). Jesus said, "Enter through the narrow gate; for the gate is wide and the way is broad that leads to destruction, and there are many who enter through it" (Matt. 7:13). He urged people to change directions, to enter the small gate that leads to the narrow way that few find. Actually, it is *Satan* who doesn't care what we believe—or how sincerely we believe it—as long as what we believe is error. The content of our faith is highly crucial. Sincerity is not sufficient. In *Mere Christianity*, C. S. Lewis makes a great analogy,

> Doctrines are like maps. They are not the reality and may not be as exciting as reality, but they chart reality for us in a vital way. Just as studying a map of the shore of the Atlantic is not as exciting as walking along the Atlantic coast itself, so studying the doctrine of atonement is not exactly the same as the experiencing the cross itself. But the purpose of a map is to represent, graph, and explain the reality. If you want to find your way, you need to have a reliable map, and we should consult it frequently.[15]

Excursus: Creeds and Confessions

Though it is beyond the scope of the present essay, C.S. Lewis' quote about doctrine functioning like maps gives me a chance to

---

[15] Lewis, *Mere Christianity*, *(New York: Harper, 2001), 119–120.*

reflect on a relatively unexplored topic in the Churches of Christ: the importance of creeds and confessions. The word "creed" comes from the Latin *credo,* meaning "I believe." A creed is an authoritative statement of basic articles of faith to which the Christian church gives assent. Since I'm arguing for a kind of triage, a metric or rubric if you will for discerning what it is that doctrinally binds us together, some might ask if it would not just be easier to make a case for the utility of creeds and confessions? After all, for those traditions that adhere to them, they are important doctrinal 'road maps' that demonstrate what is most important doctrinally.[16]

Problematically, however, creeds and confessions have often come under intense criticism in the Stone-Campbell Movement. Given that we are a people of the book, that we affirm "no creed but the Bible," isn't using creeds and confessions a bit silly to consider? Perhaps it is. But consider a vignette from the introduction of Carl Trueman's *The Creedal Imperative*:

> A colleague of mine loves to tell the following story about a church he used to visit. The pastor there had a habit of standing in the pulpit, seizing his Bible in his right hand, raising it above his head, and pointing to it with his left. "This," he declared in a booming voice, "is our only creed and our only confession." Ironically, the church was marked by teaching that included the five points of Calvinism, dispensationalism, and a form of polity that reflected in broad terms its origins as a Plymouth Brethren assembly. In other words, while its only creed was the Bible, it actually connected in terms of the details of its life and teaching to almost no other congregation in the history of the church. Clearly, the church did have a creed, a summary view of what the Bible taught on grace, eschatology, and ecclesiology; it was just that nobody ever wrote it down and set it out in public. That is a serious problem...it is

---

[16] Creeds and confessions are summaries of Christian belief. In them, we summarize our most basic convictions in ancient creeds such as the Nicene-Constantinopolitan (325, 381 AD) and the Apostles' Creed, which developed gradually from the 2nd through the 6th centuries. Our core convictions are also summarized in the Definition of Chalcedon (451 AD) and the Athanasian Creed, which, though not actually written by Athanasius, is a wonderful summary of the ecumenical or catholic (i.e., universal) doctrines of the Trinity and Christ. We call these the catholic (universal) creeds.

actually unbiblical; and that is ironic and somewhat sad, given the (no doubt) sincere desire of the pastor and the people of this church to have an approach to church life that guaranteed the unique status of the Bible.[17]

One could just as easily substitute this minister for one of our own. In his place, our minister, shouting the same criticisms of creeds and confessions, inhabits a church marked by Arminian soteriology, a congregationalist polity with a Presbyterian-born local governance by a plurality of male elders, and a view of baptism at least partly shaped by our Baptist roots –not to mention Anabaptist influences, etc. Not to suggest that our practices are not biblically rooted, of course. But I do mean to suggest that every Christian tradition has a kind of "creedal tradition" which serves both to define and delimit its view of salvation, orthodoxy, fellowship, etc. This is true even of those traditions that, like our own, radically oppose the creeds.

Perhaps it is time for the Churches of Christ to re-evaluate the functional importance of creeds and confessions in our fellowship? To begin, we might at least establish the relative importance of creedal statements within the Scriptures. Both Old and New Testaments indicate the necessity and inevitability of creedal statements in marking the true, God-revealed faith. Confessions like "Jesus is Lord" (Rom. 10:9-10) and "Yahweh is One" (Deut. 6:4) serve as theological *shibboleths* (cf. Judges 12:5-6) distinguishing the orthodox from the heterodox. In 2 Timothy 1:13, Paul emphasizes not only the conceptual content of his doctrine *but the actual form* by which that doctrine had been delivered. In that way, the scriptures lay the groundwork for an explicit confession of faith that conforms to recognized norms of doctrine and expression. The form of expression was transmitted by the Apostles to the earliest Christian communities. As Carl Trueman notes, "a case can surely be made for seeing a clear, consistent, and legitimate development from the teaching and practice of Paul in the New Testament through the Rule to the creeds of the fourth century and beyond."[18]

---

[17] Carl Trueman, *The Creedal Imperative (Grand Rapids: Crossway, 2012)*.
[18] *Creedal Imperative*, 105. For a concise overview of creedal development in the first five centuries of the Church, see pages 81-108.

Of course, the Churches of Christ do not self-identify as "confessional." We are a non-confessional people. So, how would our churches give greater credence to the importance of creeds? At the very least, we might begin by exploring the benefit of affirming the great ecumenical creeds: the Apostle's Creed, Niceno-Constantinopolitan Creed, and Athanasian Creed, particularly given our place in the American Restoration Movement, arguably the oldest ecumenical movement in America. The three Creeds listed above are called *ecumenical* (general, universal) because they have been accepted by most Christian churches. They deal with the Christian church's core beliefs, especially regarding the doctrine of the Trinity.

If you see the merit in the utility of the Creeds, let me offer some suggestions for how our 'non-confessional' churches might become more "confessional" in our thinking and practice:

1. *Value that the universal church believes and confesses important truths.* Our doctrinal statements are not merely something that one puts a checkmark beside when one becomes a member of the local church. It is a statement of faith; it is a statement of belief. You are saying, "I, with my local church body, confess and profess that these things are true and solid Biblical doctrine." Encourage your members to see how your statement of faith intersects with the wider Christian tradition.
2. *Incorporate historic Creeds into your teaching.* For example, we can regularly remind people that the things we believe—that Jesus is Lord, that he was crucified, buried and raised from the dead—are things that the church has confessed for 2,000 years. The Creeds reflect this.
3. *Incorporate the Creeds into your disciple-making process.* The ecumenical Creeds and even tools like the Heidelberg Catechism (the most ecumenical of the Protestant catechism) make excellent study guides and even devotional readings to help understand key Biblical doctrines. New and young believers need help to build a grid or framework of basic doctrines. A historic Creed (or catechism) can be an excellent aid serving as a lattice upon which their growing vine of biblical knowledge may begin.

4. *Use the Creeds in your Sunday Schools.* I have taught about the Creeds when I taught about church history. On one occasion in a Sunday school class, we spent several weeks looking at the Christological controversies in the early church and the issues that lead to the Nicene Creed and the Chalcedonian Creed. As we looked specifically at these Creeds, it was important to emphasize how these documents were biblical in their articulation but also that the language affects our church today. We confess Christ as one person having two natures that are united "inconfusedly, unchangeably, indivisibly, inseparably." We need to remember as Christians we believe and confess these things.

I realize that the idea of teaching from much less even mentioning creeds might be an intimidating thought for many of us. But don't shy away from them. They are the treasures of the Christian tradition. I raise the idea here in the hopes that others might consider their use. Perhaps these ideas might be explored more fully elsewhere.

Three Orders of Doctrine

Let us now consider a prospective list of doctrines and the way they might fall out within the three orders. For our purposes, this exercise is useful because, by identifying which doctrines are most essential, we are then able to determine what it is that is most important in holding our fellowships together theologically.

First-Order Doctrines

The set of first-order doctrines are those that are essential to the Christian faith. Denying these doctrines represents nothing less than the eventual denial of Christianity itself. However, Christians across a vast denominational range can stand together on the first-order doctrines and recognize each other as authentic Christians. Included amongst these doctrines would be such things as:

– The doctrine of the Trinity (i.e., Who God is);

- That God created all the material of creation into existence from nothing (God made the world);
- The full deity and humanity of Jesus Christ (Who Jesus is);
- That Jesus was God incarnate, lived a life of perfect obedience, died on the cross for our sins, and was bodily resurrected (How Jesus becomes Mediator between God and humanity);
- The doctrine of atonement (closely allied with the preceding point) which states that Christ's life and death canceled God's objective condemnation and Jesus bore our curse as a sacrifice for sin, so we have peace with God through Christ's blood. In His resurrection, Jesus destroyed the reign of sin and death;
- That Jesus is Lord (i.e., Jesus is ascended and reigns now over His kingdom);
- The inherent sinfulness of humanity and need for salvation (Why we need saving);
- That justification is by faith alone (the instrumental cause of our salvation);
- The inspiration and authority of Scripture (How God reveals Himself to us in special revelation);
- That a Spirit-born people of God, existing in covenant with Him, become a church for the world (the redeemed comprise the *ekklesia* of God);
- Jesus Christ will return bodily to gather His own and to judge the living and the dead.

Second-Order Doctrines

The set of second-order doctrines is distinguished from the first-order set by the fact that believing Christians may disagree on the second-order issues, though this disagreement will create significant boundaries between believers. Many Christians will organize themselves into denominational forms (Churches of Christ, Southern Baptist, Presbyterian, etc.) and the boundaries of the denomination are usually rooted in the second-order doctrines. Of course, many of the most heated debates will concern these second-order doctrines because these issues concern the church and its ordering. These would include such things as:

- The meaning and mode of baptism[19]
- Specific doctrinal issues related to theological systems, such as Calvinism and Arminianism. Though the differences will be marked and passionately defended, each camp should acknowledge the other camp as fellow believers.
- Ecclesiological and church polity concerns
- Overarching doctrines related to Christian liturgical or worship forms (e.g., issues relating to sacramental theology in general or more specifically, different understandings of the Lord's Supper)
- Issues relating to women in 'ordained' ministry

Third-Order Doctrines

Third-order issues are doctrines over which Christians may disagree and remain in close fellowship, even within local congregations. These would include such things as:

- Issues related to eschatology (i.e. timetable and sequence for Jesus' bodily return).
- In the Churches of Christ, issues relating to the debates over *a capella* worship vs. worship with musical instruments.
- In the Churches of Christ, issues relating to the distinctives of the 'non-institutional' Churches of Christ.
- Issues related to the interpretation of difficult biblical texts

There are a myriad of issues that might be added to the list of third-order doctrines. Christians may find themselves in disagreement over any number of issues. Nevertheless, standing together on issues of more urgent importance, believers are able to accept one another without compromise when third-order issues are in question.

---

[19] We in the Churches of Christ have a very high view of baptism and often disagree with other denominational understandings of it. However, others fervently disagree over basic understandings of baptism, too (for example, Baptist and Presbyterians). I am suggesting that even though we disagree fundamentally over each other's views of baptism, we can acknowledge this difference as we organize denominationally, and yet, we can still accept one another as fellow believers.

Conclusion

In this essay, I have a proposed an exercise—a kind of theological triage to help us determine in the Churches of Christ what it is that is most important doctrinally and theologically speaking. The proposal is unapologetically doctrinal. Doctrine proves as indispensable to Christianity as a skeleton to the body or oxygen to breathing. Without Christian doctrine, believers would be stripped of truth. The New Testament epistles overflow with exhortations to make "sound doctrine" the very heart of Christian faith and ministry.[20]

In the 21st century, the Churches of Christ will continue to consider how we can confess Christ in the light of the impressive challenges inside and outside of the church. As we look to the past, we see that faithfulness to the message and the mission of Christ on the basis of his Word and in dependence on his Spirit led the post-apostolic church to develop refined creedal statements. The results of that era were the Nicene-Constantinopolitan Creed (focusing on the dogma of the Trinity); the Chalcedonian Definition (concentrating on the person of Christ); and the Athanasian Creed (summarizing the catholic faith). Despite continued eruptions of discord through the centuries and widespread criticism in the modern era, these conclusions reached in the first five centuries created a consensus that has remained the touchstone of Christian confession to the present day. Creeds are not an important part of our tradition. But they could be, and perhaps they should be. For many other traditions, the creeds help "bind the center."

This essay has considered what is most important to the Christian faith, what I have called "first-order doctrines." The first-order doctrines are those that are essential to the Christian faith. When we consider what is most important for us theologically, we are considering these kinds of doctrines. I have proposed a handful of doctrines without which I think it impossible to have the Christian

---

[20] We are reminded by Paul: (1) To be a good minister of Christ Jesus, brought up in the truths of the faith and of the good teaching (1 Tim 4:6); (2) What you heard from me, keep as the pattern of sound teaching (2 Tim 1:13); (3) Preach the Word (2 Tim 4:2); (4) Hold firmly to the trustworthy message... encourage others by sound doctrine (Titus 1:9); and (5) Teach what is in accord with sound doctrine (Titus 2:1). Just imagine where the gospel would be if Paul had not publicly confronted Peter over faulty doctrine (Gal 2:11–21).

faith. Some theological diversity and debate will always be necessary, but the first-order doctrines represent that which is vital. Let it be these things that bind us.

Finally, it is important that I address the topic of why I have stayed in the Churches of Christ as a minister and theologian. As I shared with another minister recently, the answer is "because I love God's people in the Churches of Christ." And I do. But also, I believe there is a tremendously important time of church renewal happening in our tradition —a movement in which there are still many more questions than there are answers. Who will we be? What are we becoming? And how does this cohere with who we have been and where we have come from? What does it mean to say "we" anymore? Despite our beginnings as a unity movement, some years ago our tradition lapsed into an extreme sectarian exclusivism. Providentially, the Churches of Christ are in the midst of something of a renaissance of grace as our scholars and theologians lead our universities and congregations away from this sectarianism back towards a grace-laden theology and ecumenism inspired and informed by the larger Christian Tradition and the gospel of Jesus Christ. My hope is that the gospel and the Tradition are renewing our tradition. But we need to have profound discussions about what "binds the center" as I have proposed. As a minister and scholar, I hope to be a part of these discussions, Lord willing.

I Stayed for the Charity

Steven C. Hunter[1]

My earliest memory of attending church was with my paternal grandfather in a Baptist Church just outside Nashville, Tennessee. The Hunters have been Baptist, I suppose, since shortly after entering the New World in the mid-eighteenth century. My great-great-grandfather, John Anderson Hunter, operated a singing school for children, and my paternal grandfather still sings in the choir of his Baptist church. In my early, formative years, I knew nothing other than what the Baptist tradition taught me.

The first time I worshiped in a Church of Christ was around the age of nine when my mother was dating who would become my stepfather. I remember asking upon entering the auditorium (sanctuary), "Mom, where's the choir going to be?" Looking back now, I realize how silly a question that was, but I did not know any difference at the time. I would be twelve when at that congregation's church camp my uncle, my step-father's brother, would explain to me that I needed to be saved and what all that entailed. Since I had such a great admiration of and trust in him, and since what he told me made complete sense, I obeyed the gospel and was immersed into Christ with one uncle taking my confession, and another uncle immersing me in the creek at Taylor Christian Camp in rural Kentucky.

Being a minister was not in the plan for me as far as I was concerned, but God, through series of events, provided me with

---

[1] Steven Hunter (PhD, Faulkner University) is the preaching minister of the Glendale Road Church of Christ in Murray, KY.

the opportunity to study and become better versed in the Scriptures in preparation for the ministry. He also opened doors for me to preach and grow, and now in my eleventh year of ministry, I find that I am well adjusted to ministry. However, there have been many times that I have wanted to quit the ministry and especially the Church of Christ.

As I have pondered my main source of frustration, I might best sum it up by pointing to hermeneutical issues and the rigidness on the part of some to hold certain matters as if they were of greater importance than larger issues. In our fellowship, many have tithed mint, dill, and cumin to the neglect of the weightier matters of the law: love, justice, and mercy. Our brotherhood has a proclivity to bind matters of liberty as matters of salvation, and we also often poorly exegete the Bible. The conclusions we arrive at are born from sincere desires, I might suggest, to please God and be faithful in His eyes, and this is a sentiment we might all view as laudable. However, no matter how well one is intentioned, such binding and misinterpretations are not without problems. Therefore, from my viewpoint, I should like to propose a middle ground, or center, for our theology, but, first, we must be completely honest with ourselves about our handling of Divine Scripture up to this point before we can see the need for a middle ground.

Binding Where God Has Not Bound

One particular sentiment adhered to by many is, "In all things, love." This statement was one part of the tripartite motto heralded by many in the Stone-Campbell Movement. The first two parts, "In doctrine, unity; in opinion, liberty," birthed the finale that in all things, we ought to conduct ourselves with love toward one another. We who advocate no confession of faith or creed must admit that such mottos border along the creedal and confessional as much as, "Speak where the Bible speaks and be silent where the Bible is silent" does. However, we've neglected to allow liberty to prevail in matters of opinion because many of our preachers have typically inferred and deduced from the Bible certain conclusions on moral and pious issues that they lay upon brethren as measures of orthodoxy. Our "mottos" are our creeds, and we sometimes refuse to acknowledge it. Furthermore, I fear, we have neglected to be loving in all things and adopted a radical Biblicism bordering on that of the ancient Pharisees. This is not at all to suggest that the Bible does not issue commands and restrictions, but we often have a lot to say wherever the Bible is silent.

For example, 1 Corinthians 6:19 urges that we as individual Christians regard our bodies as temples of God in which the Spirit dwells. From this passage and an interpretation of it, many preachers and Bible teachers have used the verse and concept of our body as a temple to denounce smoking as something that is sinful. The premise given is that if our body is the temple, we should not want to defile the temple (our body) by putting something damaging into it such as that which excretes from tobacco—something that experts have identified as hazardous to one's health.

Is this particular interpretation all that burdensome? Does this one issue create anxiety for a Christian? For those who do not smoke, no. However, I'm not at all suggesting that this is *the* matter that has caused frustration, but many like it. When you take a bunch of issues in this same vein using poor and inconsistent hermeneutics, concluding that the outcome is a heaven and hell issue, it would appear that Christianity has become more about manipulation or coercion by certain schools of thought[2] and those that adhere to them than conforming to the image of Christ. If you would like to hold to this interpretation, well and fine, but don't try to force it on others so that they fit into your definition of righteousness when that very definition may not be one identifiable to God.

Speaking about hermeneutical inconsistency, I press on to when one is forced to defend the premise given of 1 Corinthians 6:19 as mentioned. Those who often interpret that passage in the way given above seldom use it to say that one shouldn't overeat, drink sodas, take pharmaceutical drugs, be inoculated, or other such things related to what one puts in the body that could be harmful either short- or long-term. This passage and the principle derived from it is applied only to smoking, at least as far as this author has experienced. While you and I may agree that smoking is harmful to one's overall well-being and unwise to partake of, we

---

[2] Such schools of thought can either derive from a school of preaching, university, publication, preacher, or a combination of several from each category.

may also concede that the majority of us likely overindulge in eating or some other harmful substance (e.g., sodas). Due to our indulgences and their ability to harm our overall health in due course, we might rather like to dismiss this hypocrisy of ours by comparing the effects of tobacco to the "minimal" damage in comparison from our substance of choice and feel better about our choices. Sadly, though, one who has a genetic predisposition to heart disease would be wiser to avoid the diet that is conducive to accelerating that destructive process. However, since no government agency has come out against fried, fatty foods, we too remain silent only because of the lack of a surgeon general's warning.

We may, as individual Christians, think this an accurate interpretation of Paul's body-temple passage and find it to be our conviction that we should not indulge in tobacco as fulfilling this verse. One may interpret the passage however they want to, given their frame of reference, but do we have the right to bind this on another Christian? I don't believe so when we study the topic in greater depth rather than skimming a surface. If other passages could contradict the interpretation given, one would be wise to give them heed in the chance that misinterpretation has occurred.

When looking at the overall context in which Paul penned his words, we may discern that he might not have had in mind the very conclusion reached and preached by our brethren. Paul was writing about sexual immorality and invoked the body as the temple to demonstrate that what one does outside their body (sexual immorality) defiles it, not what they put into it since both stomach and food will both be destroyed (1 Corinthians 6:13). Furthermore, Jesus even stated that what one puts into his body did not defile him, but what proceeded from the heart did (Matthew 15:10–11). The argument could also go further and point to the fact that since tobacco grows from seeds and God created such for our nourishment (Genesis 1:11–12, 29), consumption in some part is not sinful at all, but overindulgence may be sinful as is gluttony and drunkenness.

Since we have been all too eager to bind where the Scriptures have not, we also misread the Scriptures with our contextual baggage. Such baggage that we bring to reading the Scriptures is usually our 21st-century Western perspective all the while forgetting that the Bible is itself an ancient Eastern text. We may confess that emptying oneself of all presuppositions is impossible, but we can seek to approach the text with as much objectivity as possible and strive to read it how the ancients read it. Our modern readings of the Bible were born out of rational, critical, scholarly examination of the text. Would the ancients have read the Bible that way? One need only to look to Augustine's *On Christian Doctrine* for an example of how earlier Christians read the Bible. Though removed from the first century by over 400 years, his understanding of Scripture may be better suited than a reading born from the baggage of one who lives 1,900 years beyond the writing of the text. After all, our interpretive tradition has filtered to us largely from the baggage associated with Stone-Campbell hermeneutics—direct command, approved example, and necessary inference.[3]

Our misreadings have often been numerous because we read our cultural presuppositions back into the text. One example is in Acts 2:42 and the mentioning of "prayers" which, in Greek, is "the prayers." Prayers as something generic is how we have often understood and applied this part of the passage. However, as is later shown in Acts (cf. Acts 3:1; 10:1–3, 9), "the prayers" had to do with the liturgical hours of prayers carried over from Judaism and likely consisting of praying particular Psalms. The early Christians whom we desire to emulate would have prayed at 6 and 9 a.m., noon, and 3 p.m. This is not anything we equate with New Testament Christianity when we preach it. Rather, we have seemed to reduce New Testament Christianity to how one is saved (soteriology), how the church is organized, and how the church worships God (ecclesiology) and that in a modern context without an entirely ancient understanding. Acts, however, entails these, but a constant theme of the church is that she is a community of prayer, not of politics, spectrums of left, right, conservative, liberal. She is much more than what we've made her out to be these days.

One main peeve of mine has been my love-hate relationship with giving an invitation at the end of every sermon. Some sermons are an invitation in themselves, while others, such as a sermon on comforting the grieving, can seem out of place once an invitation is tagged on at the end. Furthermore, most brethren begin packing

---

[3] The influences of these have been well documented as Lockean and others of the Scottish Enlightenment.

up and make the awfullest noise so that anyone who might contemplate responding is so distracted and led to believe that we don't take it seriously so they shouldn't either. Quite honestly, I never read about a sermon in the New Testament where an invitation was offered and a hymn was sung. The informed reader will know that this arose out of the Great Awakening and Second Great Awakening and is an offspring of the altar call during those revivalist periods. There's certainly nothing wrong with an invitation, but it isn't biblical and we who preach that we are biblical ought very well to be so or stop saying we are when we have such an innovation, regardless how laudable it may be.

Brethren have questioned my orthodoxy because I don't offer invitations at the end of every sermon. I confess that I do not desire to do things in a "Church of Christ" way, nor am I faithful to the "Church of Christ" per se. I am, however, a Christian, and I love Christ's bride, but we have to realize how much of what we hold so dear is often mistaken as sound when in reality it's cultural. Again, there's nothing at all wrong with it, but it ought to never be *bound* upon another if it's of us and not the Lord, and the binding of such a tradition has been a thorn in my side.

For those who share these frustrations, I'm sure we could all sit around and vent to one another. We might even feel a little bit better after having done so. In the midst of it all, while it is good for one to get things off one's chest, constant griping may lead us to have hearts and minds that please Satan more than God, and we realize that we wouldn't want to do that. I have spent time licking my wounds, shouting from the rooftops, and strutting my rhetorical superiority to those less enlightened than I when so challenged. I have also begun to heal, and a large part of that healing process, for me, has been to give to others the very thing I desire from them—grace.

Being Charitable

As noted above, there have been many reasons and frustrations that I could have used as an excuse to leave the Church of Christ. Why have I stayed? Were I ever to find the perfect church and go there, I would mess it up. The very frustrations I have with others, and the way things are done are the product of our carnal nature.

Our fallen, carnal nature is prone to cause and be frustrated by such issues. I would only be leaving problems rather than contributing to solutions. If I perceive that there are issues that exist, I can pick up my ball and play elsewhere, or I can try to contribute to correcting the very issues I see in the hopes of inspiring others to do the same. What if Hezekiah and Josiah had never tried to make things better? What if Ezra and Nehemiah left the walls torn asunder? What if Jesus never came? If I am unable to contribute to solutions and make things better, ought I not to have more patience with my brethren and receive them in the Lord rather than disputing over scruples (Romans 14)?

If I want others to give me liberty in my views, I have to be willing to give the same. If I want brethren to treat me lovingly despite our differences, I must be willing to do the same. We are to bear with one another if we should have a complaint against others (Colossians 3:13). We who think ourselves strong ought to bear with the weak (Romans 15:1), and we're to receive the weaker brethren not to debate over issues, but in fellowship with Christ. Who's to say that I am not the weak one while thinking it's others who are weak?

If I were less diligent in Bible study, or even less educated, I might and have viewed the issues of my frustration similarly to those in whom I find grief. Just because I may have greater depth of knowledge of the Scriptures and such matters, I ought not to be boastful, because knowledge puffs up, but love edifies (1 Corinthians 8:1). It has always been easy for me to find, note, and proclaim the faults of another. What's often harder, but more necessary, is that I point that same critical eye at myself. I was once where they are, and God was patient with me, so I need to be patient with others no matter what. The charity a Christian desires from a fellow believer is the same charity that ought to be given, and this is why I have stayed.

Examining Our Hermeneutic

The above are examples of the hermeneutic some of our brethren use to lead them to teach that the Bible can give us a "thus sayeth the Lord" for *everything* about life. We see such tracts and pamphlets directed to Christian ethics on topics of smoking, going to prom, dancing, and various other issues considered to be moral issues and then the views stated are believed and bound upon others, and what results is the judging of our brethren and their love of God and the truth. When we do this, we have made our inferences and deductions as good as doctrine just as the Pharisees did of their traditions. In so doing, we have found an area in which we test another's orthodoxy, and if they are found wanting in the area, we mark them, and then hold them as brethren in error, at best, or bound for eternal damnation, at worst.

Barton W. Stone and Alexander Campbell differed on many points, yet, despite such, they were able to move toward a consensus of unity. Restoration historians have written at length about their union and differences, so I would urge the reader to pick up such books since this is not our goal here. To briefly mention one difference, Stone believed and preached believers immersion, but did not bind it while Campbell saw it as a necessity. Stone would call one who had been baptized as an infant his brother or sister while Campbell would not. Stone did not want to make this point a matter of fellowship, but Campbell did.

The later movement, after their deaths, rested in part upon positive law—anything expressly stated was to have been followed while anything not so mentioned was prohibited—as restrictive to only what was commanded while some thought silence from a positive law was permissive. A battle between what the silence of the Scriptures meant ensued. The difference of hermeneutics ultimately led to mission societies and instrumental music, though the discussion on these two had existed in the antebellum period. Those in favor of each believed the Scripture's silence permitted them while those who viewed differently believed innovating where there was scriptural silence to have been an issue of adding to the Word of God.

One thing I believe we may be able to agree on is that if the Bible says we ought to do or not do something, then that is as good as clear. However, even this principle is not without problems because Paul concludes many of his letters by urging that the brethren greet one another with a holy kiss, which we might understand as an Eastern cultural exchange. Nevertheless, the point can still stand that if commanded or expressly forbidden, we ought to do or not do according to the Word of the Lord while also discerning what was for their time and what is universal and timeless.

I might also, as Campbell would agree, urge that we not bind upon others any inferences or deductions, regardless how logical and reasonable they may be. Some may, in fact, be necessary inferences, but Campbell once argued that creeds were themselves the product of human reasoning, inferences, and deductions. Since he and Stone heartily rejected creeds, he urged that inferences be matters of private interpretation and piety. After all, two men could read the same inspired text, infer, and come to contradictory conclusions. They were able to do so because of "the prejudices of education, habits of thinking, modes of reasoning, different degrees of information, the influences of a variety of passions and interests, and above all, the different degrees of strength of human intellect."[4] All too often have I been frustrated by having certain things bound upon me when I have held a different opinion.

There was a time when even notable preachers in Churches of Christ differed on the medium of the indwelling of the Spirit. They would debate such in open forums but walk off the stage still brethren. There seem to be fewer brethren who would allow for such differences, but would insist that if certain matters aren't viewed as consistent with their interpretation that the opponent would then be guilty of rejecting the truth. One of the worst things to come out of disagreements over doctrinal matters has been *ad hominem* attacks that are completely unwarranted and unnecessary. Therefore, as proposed above, let us not bind on others what Scripture doesn't; let us respect the liberty of another's interpretation and conscience. I have stayed because, while I could have left, I still believe in the aim of Churches of Christ—to do things as the New Testament Christians did them.

A Middle-Ground Hermeneutic

To abandon inferences, which some consider necessary, would undercut some of the cherished beliefs to which we hold. For example, necessary inference allows us to protest infant baptism as well as confirm that the early Christians partook of the Lord's Supper

---

[4] *Christian Baptist* 2 (March 1825): 179–80.

on the first day of every week. One may reason that were we to abandon necessary inferences as a hermeneutical method altogether that we may have to rethink our views on these and other such issues where inference has been an aid. I confess that the inferences I would wish to abandon are not all inferences, but certainly, those which are wrought from poor logic and read into the Text rather than from it. They would also lead to confessions of faith and creeds, which are no evil in themselves as long as private interpretation can judge them and discern differently. Without inferences altogether, we could not say that the preaching of Christ entailed preaching the necessity of baptism (Acts 8:35–36).

I propose that we adopt something like a Ferguson Hermeneutic. Everett Ferguson of Abilene Christian University has demonstrated erudition in Scripture and early church history. His books *Early Christians Speak*[5] demonstrate a familiarity with scriptural practices of early Christians and couple those with what early Christian literature says on the matter. He also highlights where in early church history changes of practices began such as baptism by immersion versus sprinkling or pouring. Sometimes the direct quotations from early Christian sources further elaborate how early Christians comprehended such matters as worship, ecclesial organization, and salvation as well as a host of other subjects.

For us in churches of Christ to attain a better consensus of what the Scriptures intend to convey, we should not ignore early Christian history. However, we must also beware that we do not read history back into the Bible, a common temptation with such an approach. In the uncertain world of interpretation, the early church's comments on, say, John 3:5 help us to understand that, as Ferguson has noted, this passage was the most utilized baptismal passage in the second century.[6] If a rather large consensus revolves around a certain passage from early Christians, we may take them as authorities—much in the same way a scholarly consensus is reached—in a sense on how the apostles would have taught the passage.

---

[5] Vol. 1, 3d. ed (Abilene: Abilene Christian University Press, 1999); Vol. 2 (Abilene: Abilene Christian University Press, 2002).

[6] Everett Ferguson, *Baptism in the Early Church: History, Theology, and Liturgy in the First Five Centuries* (Grand Rapids: Wm. B. Eerdmans, 2009), 143.

This method, however, does not suggest that we read all of Ferguson's writings to understand Scripture properly, but that we take his method as presented in *Early Christians Speak*. His approach uses church history to solidify good biblical interpretation while also rejecting wild notions that we allow to divide us—such as eating on church grounds as poorly exegeted from 1 Corinthians 11:20–22, or believing in a word-only indwelling of the Spirit which cannot be found as a viable interpretive tradition in early Christianity. Since the early Christians would not have interpreted the passage this way, and since their pneumatology would have likely never allowed for a word-only indwelling, we can reject such fallacious notions right from the start and ask what it was they believed about such.

The Stone-Campbell Movement and we who are associated with conservative branches in them have long advocated a return to New Testament Christianity. A part of this return, I offer, is to not only be saved, organized, and worship how ancient Christians did but that we learn to think like them too. They would have been well-versed in the Septuagint rather than the Hebrew Old Testament. They interpreted Scripture Christologically and allegorically. They were also familiar with apocryphal and pseudepigraphical writings, the book of Enoch being rather popular among them. Such things we have left to scholars, but they were a part of the life of the church then.

Conclusion

I do not at all want to seem a change agent. That is furthest from my heart and mind. Rather, I would wish that we would adopt an even more ancient approach to our biblical interpretation than we tend to in twenty-first century America. Those who came before us wanted to unite all believers in Christ, but before we could take up this mantle again, we must heal the divides among us so far as we can.

While the temptation to leave Churches of Christ may exist in the minds of some, we must understand that no tradition is without its flaws—even those with a unified theology (e.g., Orthodoxy). Nevertheless, while I could have left, I stayed for the charity with which many of my views expressed herein have already been met with welcome. I stayed because a lot of the frustrations of interpretation are beginning to come to light and brethren are rethinking how we have interpreted the Bible. I stayed because it requires charity on my part towards others, and so many have already given me such charity.

I Stayed for the Water

Grant B. Sullivan[1]

Introduction

I hope I never forget the day I was "baptized into Christ." It was a Saturday morning just before lunchtime. I was 19 years of age and had been considering it for a couple of months. I had called several family members and the local preacher Milton. I had spent weeks studying and asking an array of questions. I'm sure some of the people I was talking things over with wondered if my interrogation would ever cease. Several friends of mine suggested baptism wasn't really all that important, while others were telling me it meant everything. What was the truth? What did I need to understand in order to make the right choice? Did it even matter what I believed? It was almost as though I was learning a new language and a new way of thinking all at the same time. It seemed to be the most important thing I had ever considered in my entire life. Could I afford to get this one wrong?

I felt a fear come over me as I witnessed how clear some people thought Scripture was concerning baptism, and yet I honestly

---

[1] Grant B. Sullivan has been preaching since 2005, with most of that time spent in his hometown of Bixby, Oklahoma. Grant received his M.Div. from Oklahoma Christian's Graduate School of Theology. He continues to enjoy reading works that challenge him to grow deeper in his understanding of God and what it means to love God and neighbor in practical ways. Grant currently serves as the preaching minister for the North Heights Church of Christ in Bixby, OK. Alongside this work's editor, Benjamin Williams, Grant is the co-host of the Low Church Lectionarian Podcast.

struggled. I recall thinking at the time, "If it is so easy to comprehend, why are there so many different answers?" The belief that people were dishonest or didn't really care what was in the Bible never satisfied me because the love and commitment I noticed in all these various individuals did not show a lack of care for God's will. One thing I definitely began to see was that in some way the waters of baptism were in the plan of God, and so to that fledgling understanding and trust, I moved forward toward the baptistery. Even though I have gained a much deeper understanding concerning baptism over the years, I have never regretted that decision for even a moment. I'm not sure I could even explain what I knew for certain about baptism on May 11th, 1996, but what I do know is I wanted to please God and be a disciple of Jesus Christ.

Your own story may be different from my own, but I hope mine is something you can relate with to some extent. I imagine if you are a minister in Churches of Christ you likely share with me a language and understanding of salvation and baptism. I for one am not ashamed of our talk, but I do wish we developed a bit more depth in the conversation about conversion. In fairness, every group of people develops their own language or way of referring to things over time that is to a certain degree unique among them. For instance, a group of friends who experience a life event together are likely to have insider conversations about the occasion years later that may sound strange to an outsider. In religion, it is often no different. While some will talk about the day they "got saved" others refer to the day they "asked Jesus to come into their heart." For the person associated with the Churches of Christ, the conversation most familiar is likely either to mention the day they "obeyed the gospel" or "were baptized." I am hopeful that insiders understand what we mean by this. My fear is that not everyone does and so our language is being re-translated by listeners in such a way that does not accurately depict salvation as well as we would hope. Put another way; we might assume everyone is on the same page and feel greater detail is unnecessary. However, this is likely not the case in many instances. Regardless, these are my people, and I understand their language about salvation better than I would other movements.

I greatly appreciate the desire we have among us to please God and obey what the Lord commands. I am proud of the devotion we have to study the Scriptures. I am thankful to have the blessing of serving as a minister among Churches of Christ where I was able to start my walk of faith as a new Christian. Still, I am painfully aware that many of our ministers are struggling to deal with some of the challenges and perceived inconsistencies in the way people are treated among us and by us concerning certain doctrines of the faith. Some have become seemingly ashamed and apologetic about some things practiced and taught in our congregations and schools. Several ministers have left ministry outright in this frustration, while others have chosen the path to move on to other traditions to continue serving in ministry. There are a number of reasons and subjects that contribute to this problem. My assignment here is to raise the question "Is there anything compelling about our teaching concerning baptism that should cause a person to "tap the brakes" before they look for perceived greener pastures to do ministry? To ask it another way, "Do Churches of Christ offer a unique and valuable understanding on the doctrine of baptism that provides a significant reason to stay?" In this chapter, I first lay out a very general view of what we believe about baptism, and acknowledge some of the common complaints I hear from some ministers and members among us. Next, I make a plea for not overreacting and jettisoning the largely positive influence and opportunity that can be found by staying among the Restoration heritage. Finally, I make an appeal that even with the acknowledgment of areas of concern the positives of our understanding are needed among believers in Jesus, and therefore ministers have every opportunity to make a difference in the world for God by remaining among us.

What We Believe

First, we need to express what people who identify simply as Christians among what is referred to as "Churches of Christ" actually believe about baptism. This is easier said than done because of some existing variations due to our strong beliefs in congregational autonomy. However, what follows should give a decent understanding and be familiar to most who identify with the Restoration Movement.

Baptism is directly associated with the gracious act of Jesus in his ministry, death, burial, and resurrection. It is believed that all people reach a point where they are able to understand right from wrong. When they do wrong (sin) they are in need of the saving work of Christ. Baptism is seen as the way in which Scripture shows individuals responding in faith and showing their commitment to being a disciple of Jesus. As Jesus died, was buried, and resurrected, so the believer comes to a point of dying to the old way of life, are lowered into a grave of water (immersion), and raised up from the water to live the new life in Christ. Although some disagreement exists on the exact manner in which the Holy Spirit is received, most agree that such happens in one form or another in connection with baptism in water. It is also often emphasized that the baptized person has been added by God to the Church (Acts 2:47). I have often heard it expressed that the person being baptized comes into contact with the saving blood of Jesus through water baptism. In this way we are sacramental, that is that God works in a mysterious way through the waters of baptism, even if we rarely use the terminology.

Everett Ferguson has written extensively on the subject of baptism and greatly helps explain our beliefs about baptism. He suggests that baptism is associated with several important concepts connected with a person's conversion. Ferguson explains that baptism is associated with a confession of faith, an act of repentance, the moment at which God pronounces the forgiveness of sins, the typical order by which the Holy Spirit is received, a new birth, connected to the death and resurrection of Jesus, and the moment in which a person is identified with the church of God.[2] As I have already acknowledged, no one person or publication can fully express the variations among us, but this is meant to serve as a general understanding that is most common.

---

[2] Everett Ferguson, *The Church of Christ: A Biblical Ecclesiology for Today*, 179-95. In addition to this work, Ferguson also has a comprehensive work on the subject called *Baptism in the Early Church* which is a great source for a deeper understanding of much that shapes our baptismal theology and practice.

Acknowledging Frustrations: Reasons some Leave

Although the emphasis of this article and the work of this project as a whole is to provide positive and helpful reasons to stay committed to our Restoration heritage, it is also important to acknowledge some of the struggles and conversations that are causing some intelligent and gifted ministers to look for greener pastures for ministry. Even though I truly believe our view of baptism is a strength, a few pitfalls exist.

First, admittedly it is a bit disconcerting that our primary language of salvation seems to emphasize talking about baptism over talking about Jesus Christ. While I realize many of my friends would quickly deny this or claim that speaking about the former implies the latter, I would say in response our language still gives us away on what we are most focused upon. When we speak primarily about the day we were baptized while avoiding language of coming to faith in Jesus Christ, something seems wonky. This is just one case where a reaction against the minimizing of baptism by some followers of Christ has created what some would claim is an uncomfortable and unnecessary overemphasis. Rather than hiding the controversies among us, in hope they will disappear, I feel we would be better served to create and maintain an environment that allows for open discussion in loving ways. In regards to baptism, it is important to acknowledge that many ministers and members alike have become disillusioned with an over-emphasis of a ritual in a way that to them is void of careful teaching of the underlying theology of baptism in the plan of God. Whether the reader agrees with the complaint does not change the reality that some are troubled over this. To minimize their concern and assume the worst is neither fair nor helpful. Conversations need to be held in loving ways. Clearer understandings should be shared and considered. However, the pertinent questions for this article remains, "is this a good reason to leave?" To what will you run, and have you considered the baggage you will claim concerning water in the plan of God among the new group you will land amongst?

Another thing that is bothersome for some is that baptism as often taught in a series of steps to salvation, seems to leave the appearance of a legalistic checklist of faith that does not neatly line up with the disciples we read about in Scripture. The order of hearing, believing, repenting, confessing, and being baptized to become a disciple has some warrant, but what about Cornelius (Acts 10) in which the receiving of the Holy Spirit came before water baptism? What are we to say about Apollos (Acts 18:24-28) and those in Ephesus (Acts 19:1-7) that had to be taught more clearly but were already considered disciples? We may admit tendencies in the texts of conversion, but we also see some variations as well. The lack of acknowledging this truth alone is another source of contention for some, while for others this list seems to be placing too much emphasis on what the human does and minimizing what God does in salvation. The concern is our approach has the earmarks of a human works-based salvation.

Furthering the frustrations of some are the quick answers that almost imply a disdain for anyone who would dare question what to them is so easily explainable. Statements like, "we all know the answer to that argument is…", while figuratively, if not literally, rolling our eyes will not help. The suspicion that exists among us at times produces an unhealthy environment where people do not ask questions for fear of rejection. I have witnessed this attitude among people on both sides of the fence. This is but another reason some become exhausted with the bickering and call it quits. But again I ask, how does baptism fit into this greater conversation of concern? Is there a compelling reason to leave over our teaching on baptism? If so, what are the primary reasons for such a serious and decisive reaction? In other words, what is so upsetting about the Restoration teaching concerning baptism that would cause you to leave?"

Perhaps the most divisive reason of all is based upon a perceived exclusivism among us that claims only our precise view and practice of baptism is truly authentic enough to be considered valid. The implication is essentially only people from our movement can have any real assurance of salvation in Christ. This view is based on the idea that all other Christian movements mess up regarding either the purpose, mode, or subject of baptism. Put more plainly, it is thought that we are unique in teaching faithfully that baptism is "for the remission of sins", that it is by immersion in water, and that it is intended as a response of a believer to the gospel and therefore not for infants. The pushback from within is that we sound arrogant and give the impression that our baptisteries are better than others. For some, our assumptions place us in the position of determining who is in and out of the kingdom. In fairness, I would ask, what of these three basic understandings would you find objectionable? If you could remove yourself from determining who is in or out of the saving blood of Jesus, would the basic teaching concerning baptism among Churches of Christ bother you? If so, in what way? What better understanding exists concerning purpose, mode, or subject? If you could hold these teachings as being the most faithful understanding without it being necessary to condemn others in their honest attempt to live by faith in Jesus Christ, would you be more at peace with your connection to the Restoration Movement?

This just scratches the surface of the many variations of complaints I have experienced in conversations among us. However, these are meant to serve as an example of the kind of things troubling some of our ministers and members. The next section of this chapter will attempt to make a case for staying, and will show among other things that we have a long history of at least some diversity concerning baptism. If there has always been room for disagreement among us, why should we feel the need to leave now? An openness to desiring the truth, sharing that with others, and leaving the judgment to God is not only possible but has been experienced from the beginning of the Restoration Movement until this very day. In my opinion, our strengths outweigh any of the supposed reasons for considering a departure.

Acknowledging Strengths: Reasons to Stay

What, if anything, makes us unique and worth holding onto as compared to another movement among Christianity concerning baptism? Is there anything to staying simply because of the familiarity that allows you to relate better and teach? What follows will not fully encompass all the good reasons to continue among Churches of Christ, and the suggestions mentioned could easily be made into a series of individual articles and more fully explored. I hope to offer encouragement to frustrated ministers and members concerning the valuable strengths we have in our understanding of baptism; we can have a positive influence on the world of people around us.

While our language about salvation can be overly focused on baptism, our robust baptismal theology among "Evangelicals" is a great strength. Rather that using baptism as our primary language, we can speak the gospel first and secondarily show how baptism connects to the gospel. In other words, we have good reason to talk about "obeying the gospel" of Jesus Christ and then explaining how baptism fits that wonderful story perfectly. The death, burial, and resurrection gospel is directly connected to the waters of baptism (Romans 6). The gospel is a story of a new beginning of which water and the Spirit are connected (John 3:1-8; Acts 2). The gospel is all about the blessings found through faith in Christ, and baptism is forever connected to being in Christ (Galatians 3:27). The gospel is about salvation, and baptism is seen through Peter as the way in which an appeal is made to God (1 Peter 3:21). Is there anything that rivals baptism as being so intricately connected to the gospel? Scot McKnight, speaking to the importance of emphasizing baptism writes

> It was Paul who explained how baptism was a gospeling act. How so? Paul saw baptism as being baptized into the death of Jesus and emerging from the waters as being co-raised with Jesus Christ...The public act of baptism is in and of itself a public declaration of the saving Story of Jesus. If done right, baptism gospels the gospel in a public manner.[3]

Baptism is a means of grace even if we must admit there is a certain level of mystery with it. I may never comprehend how God meets humans with the cleansing blood of Jesus in the waters of baptism, but I do not need to understand it fully to accept its reality by faith. Among us, a person has room to view baptism in a sacramental way that is appealing even if some might shy away from the word sacrament itself. Much like our commitment to the importance of the Lord's Supper, we also have continued with baptism even when it was not popular. True, we may be dissatisfied-with how we argue for it based almost solely upon the biblical ex-

---

[3] Scot McKnight, *The King Jesus Gospel*, 158.

ample with little effort given among many to seek a deeper understanding. Still, this commitment to these sacraments started in the roots of restoration with people like Alexander Campbell even if we do not realize it, and remain an ingrained strength of ours to this day.

Fortunately, we are now seeing a significant shift in appreciation for the historical practices and traditions of the Church. Of course, not everyone has appreciated such a view as our movement has expressed over the years. Hicks and Weedman write regarding tensions among Southern Baptists that have been expressed which serves as an example of the impact our sacramental tendencies concerning baptism have had on other movements. They share "the Campbellites injected a sacramental virus into the Baptists for which they have not yet developed an immunity!"[4] What might be intended as a negative shot fired our direction actually lands as a diamond of great value. To stay is to remain a part of a movement that has had and continues to have a positive impact on the larger Christian movement as a whole. Though we are small in number, our influence has significant effect with the help of God.

Therefore, while it is true that Evangelicalism is most often all about the head (heart) but ignores the importance of responding in the body, our movement is able to shed some light on what is a more balanced approach and avoids the side that seems to disregard the body in an almost gnostic approach. Curt Niccum mentions this kind of "stark dualism introduced by Gnostics and others overly influenced by Greek philosophies of the day [which] resulted in some heretical groups separating 'spiritual' activity from "physical" elements."[5] This conversation is nothing new. Caneday writes:

> When speaking of God's salvation in Jesus Christ, failure to distinguish the means from the ground, or instrument from basis, or intermediary cause from efficient cause wreaks havoc in Christian theology, in the church, and in the lives of individuals within the church. Some Christians, zealous to guard God's grace against any intrusion of works, regularly confuse faith and grace...they carelessly speak of faith as the basis of

---

[4] Hicks and Weedman, *Believer's Baptism*, 378.
[5] Curt Niccum, *Baptism in the Restoration Movement*, 182.

salvation and isolate faith from other biblically sanctioned means… Regrettably, confusion of instrumental cause and efficient cause leads some to regard baptism as itself accomplishing regeneration, and others to make baptism optional, with little, if any, meaning.[6]

In his time Alexander Campbell had to answer his own critics such as a Baptist from Virginia named Andrew Broaddus. "Broaddus reduced baptism to a mere external bodily act or a simple mutual pledge by which people are received into the visible church…Whereas for Broaddus the exercise of faith is wholly internal and a matter of the heart alone, Campbell believed that faith is exercised through trusting in Christ, coming to him and receiving him in the act of immersion."[7] Baptism is an act of the body (physical) but is a manifestation of divine grace. Baptism, it could be suggested, is a means by which we are able to make an appeal to God in the body in order to experience forgiveness.

Through baptism, we get a concrete moment in time that God washed away our sins. Similar to how kneeling in prayer shows the importance of remembering we are made physical and respond to God both from the heart and in the body, so baptism provides that unified action where we come to God with spirit, mind, heart, body—yes, the entireness of what God has made us to be as humans. In this way, baptism becomes a fuller response to the gospel than internal thought alone can provide. This is what Campbell was looking for in a conversion experience. Hicks shares:

> But our consciousness of forgiveness is not made to proceed from any inward impulses, voices, or operations, either instantaneous or gradual, but from a sure and more certain foundation—the testimony of God addressed to our ears. If operations, impulses or feelings, were to be the basis of our conviction, it would be founding the most important of all knowledge upon the most uncertain of all foundations. 'The heart of man is deceitful above all things,' and 'He that trusts in his own heart, is a fool.'

---

[6] A. B. Caneday, *Baptism In The Stone-Campbell Restoration Movement*, 324-25.
[7] Hicks and Taylor, *Down In The River to Pray: Revisioning Baptism as God's Transforming Work*, 137-8.

Consequently, Campbell approached the moment of baptism as the moment of objective assurance. It is an assurance based upon faith in the gospel promises rather than upon precariously interpreted subjective feelings.

> For example, I believe the testimony concerning Jesus of Nazareth in the apostolic import of it. I then feel myself commanded to be immersed for the forgiveness of sins. I arise and obey. I then receive it, and am assured of it, because God cannot deceive. Thus I walk by faith—not by feeling.[8]

We continue to have a great opportunity for helping others experience and appreciate these sacraments. We especially can help provide a reasonable claim to the importance, purpose, and value of baptism in God's plan for saving people. There is no need to wonder if you are truly a disciple when you follow the manner Jesus taught for making disciples. We stand on the right side of history in these practices, which seems to me a substantial reason to stay.

Finally, let me make an argument that the frustration mentioned previously in this chapter regarding the view that all baptisms performed by groups outside of our heritage are invalid. I do not see this as a good reason to leave. You might be asking why I would make such a statement. Have you considered the fact that this belief is not universal among our movement? In fact, this is not a new disagreement. Many preachers, leaders, and even presidents of our Universities have found themselves on both sides of this debate. It did not cause them to leave just because they had disagreements. Why should it be any different for us?

Consider the following as a small sampling of examples that serve as valuable evidence that the voice of those insisting on rebaptism do not speak for all who identify among Churches of Christ. Alexander Campbell tells of his own baptism in a dialogue format discussing rebaptism. Campbell explains that his own immersion was based upon a simple confession "that Jesus was the Messiah the Son of God."[9] He further stated, "nor have I ever immersed any person but upon the same profession which I made

---

[8] John Mark Hicks - *"God's Sensible Pledge": The Witness of the Spirit in the Early Baptismal Theology of Alexander Campbell*, p. 10-11.

[9] Alexander Campbell, *Millennial Harbinger*, 1832, p. 319.

myself."[10] For Campbell, any person who desired fellowship and was persuaded in his own mind that their immersion was a faithful and obedient response to God should not be refused a "seat in the family of God; and still less to insist upon his being immersed according to the views or for the good pleasure of others."[11] Although Campbell left room for the individual to be re-immersed if, for personal reasons, they were unsure of their prior baptism, he was convinced that the preachers of his time who were insisting on rebaptism were wrong. Campbell writes:

> I know some will say that the candidates which they immersed a second time did not rightly understand baptism the first time. Well, I am persuaded they did not understand it the second time; and shall they be baptized a third time! But did all the believers whom the Apostles baptized understand their baptism in all its designs, meaning, and bearings. We presume not, else the Apostles need not have written to them to explain it: "Know you not," said Paul to the Romans, "that so many of us as were immersed into Jesus Christ were immersed into his death."[12]

Of course, not everyone agreed with Campbell; John Thomas being the chief rival to him on this subject. According to Roderick Chestnut, Thomas "believed...baptism, if performed properly, procured salvation. For Baptism to be valid the subject, as well as the administrator, had to realize that baptism was for the remission of sins...If that knowledge was lacking it invalidated the rite, leaving the believer in his sins."[13]

The disagreement and discussion on this subject did not end with Campbell and Thomas. Later people like James A. Harding and David Lipscomb would also write on this matter. Harding felt the only thing that should be determined about a person desiring to place membership among one of our congregations is if, prior to their baptism, they believed "with the heart that Jesus is the Christ, the Son of the living God. He who demands more than this

---

[10] Ibid.

[11] Alexander Campbell, *Millennial Harbinger*, 1832, p. 319.

[12] Alexander Campbell, *Millennial Harbinger*, 1831, p. 483.

[13] Roderick Chestnut, *Baptism and the Remission of Sins: John Thomas and the Rebaptism Controversy*, 203-204.

demands too much."[14] The Gospel Advocate publication released an article by David Lipscomb in December of 1907 entitled *Rebaptism Reviewed*. This was arguably Lipscomb's most thorough discussion of the issue. The article is in response to "Brother Chism," who took the view that rebaptism was necessary.[15]

As you can see, there is a great platform for discussion of baptism that is invaluable. These conversations have not always been handled in the best of ways. I am sure love has been strained at times. Personalities tend to dominate above the actual importance of the teaching in mind if we are not careful. We should be mindful of the temptation to devour one another and give way to the desires of Satan in all of this. However, to discuss important teachings of Scripture is at the core of our history. The subject of baptism is one of our greatest discussions of all. Should we let the negative spirit that at times finds its way among us ruin the overall good we have to offer? I hope not, for I fear this is the greatest defeat of all that Satan desires most.

An Appeal to Stay

You may feel as though you are laboring in vain at times. The frustrations may never cease. However, a large part of the problem may be found within ourselves. The apostle Paul did not have things easy in his ministry. It is not as though he never faced troublemakers, bad attitudes, and stubbornness. Still, he did not give up on the churches he helped to establish. He did not so quickly remove himself from care and concern. If you are looking for the perfect church where you will not face many troubles, then beware. If such a group exists, it might be better for you to stay away so that you do not mess things up. Instead of leaving, why not dig down within all the love you have for others and give everything you have to helping the people you already know move closer to living the will of the Father. Instead of focusing on the negatives, why not spend more time thinking about the value of what we

---

[14] James A. Harding, "What a Brother Editor Thinks, With Some Comments Thereon," *The Way* 2 (July 1900) 98.

[15] David Lipscomb, "Gospel Advocate", *Rebaptism Reviewed*, December 12th, 1907.

stand for concerning baptism and other things. We have acknowledged that within our movement we are not 100% agreed upon all aspects and questions surrounding the doctrine of baptism, but how does this ruin the potential for good ministry? Further, how do you know whether you might have room to grow in your understanding along the way as well? With each passing day I find myself noticing just how much I still have to learn, and I doubt I am alone in this.

I make one final appeal to stay. First, let me remind that you are among a people that care immensely about what God has revealed to humanity through the Scriptures. I would hope you are not looking for a group that rejects the importance of learning from the texts in the Bible and diligently seeking to live the will of our Father in heaven. With that assumption in mind, we should agree that Scripture speaks of the gospel as being of first importance. The death, burial, and resurrection of Jesus Christ is the heart of our story. Jesus died to save us from our sins. It is through baptism that we are able to die, be buried, and rise to a new life. Baptism is a means of the saving grace of God being imparted to us. In this way, baptism can rightly be said to save. Second, being a Christian implies following the example of Jesus in every manner possible to the best of our ability. The Lord Jesus was baptized and since a servant is not above the Master, then how better to show my allegiance than following Christ's example through submitting to baptism? We may not see the Spirit descend as a dove, and we may not experience the audible words of the Father, but we have good reason to believe and teach others that something amazing is taking place when a person comes up from the water. Finally, baptism is solidly placed among the foundations of the faith according to Ephesians 4:4-6. The great list of "ones" that speaks of the unifying action of God includes baptism. What among these "ones" am I ready to disregard?

Water has always been in the plan of God for the Church. The history of the teaching of the Church is on our side.[16] Water should continue to be in the plan, for who are we as humans to remove it? Now is not the time to leave. Now is the time to clearly share the gospel, to call people to repentance, to teach people to follow

---

[16] For reference see, Everett Ferguson, *Baptism In the Early Church: History, Theology, and Liturgy In the First Five Centuries.*

the example of Jesus and, yes, to "go therefore and make disciples of all nations, baptizing them in the name of the Father and of the Son and of the Holy Spirit, and teaching them to obey everything that I have commanded you."[17]

---

[17] Matthew 28:19-20, NRSV.

I Stayed for the Table

Scott Elliott[1]

Man was not made for the Christian Institution, but the Christian Institution for man. (Alexander Campbell)

In the Lord's house there is always the table of the Lord. (Alexander Campbell)

The Lord's Supper has always held a prominent place within the Stone-Campbell movement. The practice of this important part of Christian worship has served as an identity marker for Churches of Christ and other groups associated with Alexander Campbell and Barton Stone. Although Churches of Christ have differed on many different subjects, there has been universal consensus on adult believers' baptism for the remission of sins and weekly observance of the Lord's Supper. Churches of Christ are not unique in emphasizing baptism and the Lord's Supper, but our beliefs and practices have often set us apart from other religious groups. The Lord's Supper is central to Sunday worship and is commonly the reason given for meeting.

In recent times, more and more religious groups have begun to emphasize the importance of baptism and the Lord's Supper.

---

[1] Scott Elliott is a graduate of Oklahoma State University and Austin Graduate School of Theology. He is married to Laura and they have two sons, Jackson and Dylan. He enjoys writing about the Christian faith and posting the occasional film review. He writes for Start2Finish blog which was recently named one of the twelve top blogs among Churches of Christ. His articles and reviews have appeared in *Relevant* magazine, *Englewood Review of Books*, and other publications.

People are rediscovering these ancient practices that Churches of Christ have continually observed and held in high regard. Churches of Christ are in a unique position to share their theology and experiences with people who are open to learning more about baptism and the Lord's Supper. Although there may be certain aspects of our past we are not fond of, now is the time to embrace our heritage and begin to have conversations with others who are intrigued by our unique beliefs.

Alexander Campbell thought highly of the Lord's Supper and devoted an entire section to this subject in *The Christian System*. For Campbell, the Lord's Supper was not just an important part of worship; it was the reason for worship itself. Although he acknowledged several biblical names for this essential act, he preferred the phrase, "breaking the loaf." In commenting on Acts 20:7 he concluded,

> [T]wo things are very obvious: 1st, That it was an established custom or rule for the disciples to meet on the first day of the week. 2d, That the primary object of their meeting was to break the loaf.[2]

Concerning this same verse, he also noted, "the most prominent object of their meeting was to break the loaf."[3] According to Campbell, the Lord's Supper was not something to be taken lightly or rushed through; it was the reason for gathering in the first place.

Throughout church history, baptism and the Lord's Supper have been described as sacraments. Campbell was not fond of the word sacrament and instead chose to use the word ordinance. Campbell listed multiple Christian practices as ordinances and believed them to be a means of grace, as well as a way of experiencing God and his salvation. He wrote,

> In the Kingdom of Heaven, faith is, then, the principle, and ordinances the means, of enjoyment; because all the wisdom, power, love, mercy, compassion, or grace of God is in the ordinances of the Kingdom of Heaven; and if all grace be in them it can only be enjoyed through them. What, then, under

---

[2] Alexander Campbell, *The Christian System*, p. 312.
[3] Ibid., p. 314.

the present administration of the Kingdom of Heaven, are the ordinances which contain the grace of God? They are preaching the gospel - immersion in the name of Jesus into the name of the Father, and of the Son, and of the Holy Spirit - the reading and teaching of the Living Oracles - the Lord's Day - the Lord's supper - fasting - prayer - confession of sins - and praise...[4]

It is evident from this statement and others that Campbell viewed the Lord's Supper as more than a memorial meal. Remembering the sacrifice of Jesus was an important aspect of the Lord's Supper, but not the only one. Campbell's theology of the Lord's Supper was rich and not one-dimensional. Campbell believed the Christian ordinances were ways of enjoying and receiving God's grace. He taught that the Lord's Supper was "well intended to crucify the world in our hearts...quicken us to God, and to diffuse his love within us."[5] He viewed baptism and the Lord's Supper as acts that contained the full power of the gospel. In the *Christian Baptist*, he wrote,

> We may say, that immersion, I mean Christian immersion, is the gospel in water, and that the Lord's supper is the gospel in bread and wine. These two ordinances of the glorious and mighty Lord fully exhibit the gospel in the most appropriate symbols.[6]

Campbell believed weekly observance of the Lord's Supper was a return to the practice of the early church, but he also saw this as shifting the focus of worship from the preacher or worship leader to God and the gospel. Since the Reformation, the sermon had become the primary focus of worship. By elevating the Lord's Supper, this would ensure that the gospel would be proclaimed every week.

Campbell also professed his belief in the presence of the Lord on the Lord's Day. He wrote,

---

[4] *The Christian System*, p. 174.
[5] *The Christian System*, p. 311.
[6] *The Christian Baptist*, vol. 5, p. 158) (*Christian Baptist*, No. 7, Vol. 5, Feb. 4, 1828.)

> The church must view herself, if sincere in her professions, as 'an habitation of God through the Spirit,' as 'the pillar and support of the truth,' as 'the temple of God,' and as 'the gate of heaven.' Every one that speaks or acts must feel himself specially in the presence of the Lord, not as on other days or in other places.[7]

Although Campbell did not associate the presence of the Lord with the elements themselves, he did believe the Lord's presence was with the congregation each time they met together on the first day of the week. This meeting was different from other gatherings on other days. It was special because Christians came together around the table in the presence of the Lord.

Christians today might not spend much time contemplating the theological reasons behind the furniture and decorations of our worship spaces, but Campbell and others who came before him did. The most significant piece of furniture for Campbell was the table.[8] His emphasis on the table is still reflected in many church buildings today. The communion table is often centrally located. It typically sits in front of the pulpit rather than behind it. The location of the table reminds worshipers of why they have gathered and the importance of the meal they will partake.

One of the most intriguing aspects of Campbell's theology of the Lord's Supper, and perhaps confusing for modern readers, is his emphasis on there being just one loaf. Churches of Christ have split over the issue of whether to use one cup or multiple cups for the fruit of the vine. At the heart of this split was a hermeneutical disagreement, but Campbell's reasoning regarding the one loaf is more theological. He argues that the one loaf represents the one body of Jesus and the one body, the church.[9] When Christians see the loaf, they are not only reminded of the body of Jesus but also of the unified body of believers. Communion is an act that not only unites us to Jesus but also to one another.

Campbell was not the only one to hold such a view concerning the one loaf. Barton Stone was in full agreement with Campbell on

---

[7] Alexander Campbell, *Millenial Harbinger Extra* No. 8 Vol. VI, October 1835, College Press p. 508.

[8] *The Christian System*, p. 304.

[9] *The Christian System*, p. 305.

this issue. He wrote, "In the Lord's supper there should be but one loaf, to represent the Lord's body that suffered on the Cross - Two or more loaves destroy the very idea of the ordinance, as not representing the one body of Christ suffering and dying."[10] Stone was equally concerned about the King James translation of 1 Corinthians 10:16-17. He felt it was misleading regarding this issue and would cause people to conclude that Christians were the one bread rather than Christ.[11]

Campbell and Stone were striving to bring attention to a practice they felt was being neglected. Some churches were observing the Lord's Supper only on a quarterly or yearly basis. Campbell and Stone believed this meal instituted by Jesus and regularly observed by the apostles needed to be an integral part of weekly Christian worship. They wished for the body of Christ to be united around the table. Stone was disappointed that Christians would divide over what he believed were petty differences regarding the Lord's Supper. He wrote,

> That the Lord's supper was celebrated and received every Lord's day by all the churches throughout the whole world, except at Rome and Alexandria is evident. These churches did not use this manner. Though they observed the ordinance on a Sunday, yet not every Sunday...Yet all the churches then lived in union, and never brought this matter into controversy. Happy should we have been, if we had done likewise; and happy should we yet be, if on this subject we be more tolerant toward each other...Of one thing I am certain; that if they affectionately remembered the Lord when they received the supper, they were right and accepted. Of another thing I am certain, they would have done wrong to have contended angrily against each other, and divided and parted asunder.[12]

Since the Reformation, many Christians had started to rethink certain aspects of Christianity. Campbell and Stones' purpose was twofold. They wished to return to the ancient order of things and bring unity to all Christians. One way of doing this was by once

---

[10] Barton Stone, *Christian Messenger*, vol. VIII no. 6, June 1834.
[11] Ibid.
[12] Barton Stone, *Christian Messenger*. vol. X no. 8, August 1836.

again making the Lord's Supper the central focus of worship. Even emphasizing the oneness of the loaf was a way of reminding all Christians that they were united although they still may disagree on certain issues. Understanding what Campbell and Stone were trying to accomplish through their teaching on the Lord's Supper is a way of understanding what they were trying to do as a movement.

These views were continued and expanded upon by Campbell and Stone's successors. Robert Milligan and Robert Richardson were both professors at Bethany College and coeditors of the *Millenial Harbinger*. Milligan penned several seminal books within the Stone-Campbell movement including *Scheme of Redemption*. Richardson wrote an influential biography of Alexander Campbell as well as other works. Both of these individuals contributed to the theology of the Lord's Supper among Churches of Christ.

In his section on the Lord's Supper in *Scheme of Redemption*, Milligan begins with a discussion of how God uses physical objects and symbols to convey a spiritual reality. He understood the Supper to be a commemorative meal, but he cautioned his readers with these words, "But to say that it is merely commemorative is not enough."[13] He goes on to write, "It is intended also to be the medium of furnishing and imparting nourishment to the hungry and thirsty soul."[14] Milligan rejected the idea of the elements of the Lord's Supper being anything other than bread and wine, but he believed the meal is more than physical food. There is a spiritual element behind the physical.

Milligan thought all the ordinances God had given his people were "a medium of nourishment to the hungry soul," but he viewed the Lord's Supper as the greatest example of this.[15] He cautioned people not to trust in "forms and shadows, in the mere rites and ceremonies of religion."[16] He wanted people to realize that God was doing more than they could see with the human eye. The Lord's Supper was not simply a physical exercise. He admitted that seeing the Lord's Supper this way "took preparation and discipline of both head and heart,"[17] but not doing so was equivalent to not

---

[13] Scheme of Redemption p. 429.
[14] Ibid., p. 429-30.
[15] Ibid., 431-32.
[16] Ibid., 432.
[17] Ibid.

partaking of the Lord's Supper at all. He asked, "How many still profess to celebrate the Lord's death who never taste of any thing more than mere symbols; who never eat the flesh nor drink the blood of the Son of God?"[18] To partake of the Lord's Supper is to receive spiritual nourishment and to miss this essential part of what God is doing is to miss out on one of the greatest blessings God has given.

Like Campbell, Milligan's understanding of the Lord's Supper was simple yet complex. They both saw this meal as being multi-dimensional. There are things God does, and there are things the participants need to do to prepare themselves for the meal. Milligan spoke of the "art and mystery of self-examination."[19] He encouraged Christians to strive to look at themselves not with a particular bias but as God himself would see them. Milligan recommended prayer and fasting in the days prior to partaking the Lord's Supper as part of the self-examination process.[20] For Milligan, this combination of spiritual nourishment and self-examination would lead to sanctification. He summed up the potential of what this meal has to offer in the following way, "But to the humble and faithful disciple who has properly examined himself, and who, through the emblematic bread and wine, really discerns and partakes of the Lord's broken body and shed blood, how exceedingly rich, and suggestive, and sanctifying in its tendencies is this most gracious ordinance!"[21]

If Campbell and Milligan provided the theology for the Lord's Supper within the Stone-Campbell movement, then Robert Richardson should be credited with laying the foundation for this moment in worship to be a time of devotion. While others were making arguments concerning the practices and beliefs related to the Lord's Supper, Richardson published a compilation of devotions and meditations entitled *Communings in the Sanctuary*. Rather than focus on the usual texts from the Gospels and 1 Corinthians that are often associated with the Lord's Supper, Richardson begins most of his meditations with a quotation from one of the Psalms. He offers an alternative to the rationalism prevalent within the

---

[18] Ibid., p. 436.
[19] Ibid., 437.
[20] Ibid., 438-39.
[21] Ibid., 441.

Stone-Campbell movement. Mystery is a common topic in his writings, and he makes statements like "the mysteries of Faith are more sublime than those of Reason."[22]

Communings in the Sanctuary opens with a question about people's understanding of the presence of God in worship. Richardson writes, "How many thus enter into the sanctuary of God, without any realizing sense of the divine presence? How many, alas, from that sleep of error never waken? Yet the Lord is in his holy temple, and will reveal himself to his people."[23] For Richardson, the "spiritual unseen" is an important aspect of worship, and something worshipers should acknowledge.[24] Worship is not just an encounter with God, but an encounter with the "unseen world."[25] Perhaps, Richardson had in mind Hebrews 12:22-24 that describes God, angels, and the great cloud of witnesses all present during worship. This takes on even greater significance when one considers Richardson offers all these comments within the context of the Lord's Supper. Not only are Christians communing with an "unseen world" but the residents of this "unseen world" are present at the table alongside them.

Richardson, like Campbell and Milligan, believed the spiritual presence of God was an essential part of the Lord's Supper and Christian worship, but he was more explicit in describing this experience than either of the other writers. For instance, "It is here that Christ himself may commune with us, and that our hearts may burn within us while we gain larger views of the mystery of redemption, and comprehend what the prophets have spoken of the sufferings of Christ and the glory that should follow. And it is here, above all, that the films of error may be taken from our eyes that we may recognize the spiritual presence of our Savior, and that he may be made known to us in the breaking of bread."[26] Richardson goes further than either Campbell or Milligan and professes that, while communing with Christ at the table, it is possible to feel one's heart burn within them. To fail to acknowledge Christ's presence during the meal was, for Richardson, tantamount to "error."

---

[22] Robert Richardson, *Communings in the Sanctuary*, p. 42.
[23] Ibid., p. 9.
[24] Ibid., p. 12.
[25] Ibid., p. 106.
[26] Ibid., 88.

One of the biggest controversies concerning the Lord's Supper within the Stone-Campbell movement was whether to have "open" or "closed" communion. Many objected to certain practices of other denominations such as only being able to partake of communion with an ordained minister present.[27] These practices were seen as barriers to observing the Lord's Supper as well as lacking Biblical justification. What emerged from the movement was a quasi-open communion where members neither invited nor banned anyone from participating.[28] Leaders wrestled with holding on to certain beliefs, such as believers' baptism for the remission of sins, while also allowing the table to be an open place where all Christians could commune. The balancing of these beliefs is evident in comments Isaac Errett made on this subject in the *Millennial Harbinger*.

1. That in primitive times there is no doubt that all who came to the Lord's table, as well as all who participated in prayer, singing, etc., were immersed believers: and we are trying to bring back that state of things.
2. But the corruptions of Popery, out of which the church has not yet half recovered, have made the people of God an erring, scattered and divided people.
3. We are pleading for further reformation; our plea proceeds on the integrity of previous pleas—it is a plea for the reunion of the scattered people of God. It does not recognize sects, on human bases, as divine; but it recognizes a people of God among these sects, and seeks to call them out.
4. We are compelled, therefore, to recognize as Christians many who have been in error on baptism, but who in the spirit of obedience are Christians indeed. (See Rom. ii. 28, 29.) I confess, for my own part, did I understand the position of the brethren to deny this, I would recoil from my position among them with utter disgust. It will never do to unchristianize those on whose shoulders we are standing, and because of whose previous labors we are enabled to see some truths more clearly than they. Yet, while fully according to them the piety and Christian standing which they deserve, it is clear

---

[27] Henry E. Webb, *In Search of Christian Unity*, p. 69, 154.
[28] Ibid.

that they are in great error on the question of baptism—and we must be careful not to compromise the truth. Our practice, therefore, is neither to invite nor reject particular classes of persons, but to spread the table in the name of the Lord, for the Lord's people, and allow all to come who will, each on his own responsibility. It is very common for Methodists, Presbyterians, etc., to sit down with us. We do not fail to teach them on all these questions, and very often we immerse them.[29]

In most cases, whether or not a person was eligible to partake of the Lord's Supper was left up to the individual. This was a very American way of handling a sticky situation. Power was taken away from the clergy/minister and given to members. Self-examination was emphasized and 1 Corinthians 11:28 was championed.

In many congregations, the minister has little or nothing to do with the communion service. In some congregations, deacons and/or elders preside over the table, but most frequently it is baptized men who offer prayers and do the serving. The Stone-Campbell movement has been an anti-liturgical movement, but this is somewhat misleading. The movement has no official liturgy and has often looked down upon groups who do, but there have been several books published that have offered an unofficial liturgy. One such volume includes instructions on how to conduct a worship service, prayers, meditations to be read before the Lord's Supper, and even sermons.[30] Although many Churches of Christ hold a high view of extemporaneous prayers and devotions, it is evident these same congregations have been significantly shaped by these informal liturgies as well as oral liturgies that have been passed from one generation to the next.

The Stone-Campbell movement's focus on the Lord's Supper has in many ways been ahead of its time. As modern Christians are rediscovering the power and importance of this meal instituted by Jesus, members of Churches of Christ have spent 200 years with the Lord's Supper being the central part of worship. Although

---

[29] Isaac Errett. "Communion with the 'Sects': Letter from I. Errett." *The Millennial Harbinger* 32 December 1861.

[30] *On the Lord's Day: A Manual for the Regular Observance of the New Testament Ordinances*, ed. by J. A. Lord, The Standard Publishing Co. 1904.

there have been disagreements regarding the theology and practice of communion, there has been universal agreement on its importance. The ties to this meal have been so strong among Churches of Christ, it has even bred peculiar practices like Sunday evening communion for anyone who missed on Sunday morning. Church members who missed morning worship make an extra effort to be present on Sunday evening for the primary purpose of taking the Lord's Supper. Personally, I believe this is a practice that should be reexamined, but it is one more example of how this meal has been held in high regard.

There is much to commend regarding the theology and practice of the Lord's Supper within the Stone-Campbell movement. The leaders of this movement sought to unite Christians around the table of the Lord. They recognized the power and influence of the sermon but also understood that worship should be centered around the presence of God encountered during communion. Although this was seen primarily as a memorial meal, the early leaders of this movement believed it was something more. They replaced the word sacrament with ordinance, but clearly viewed it as a means of grace. It was where the believer came to receive spiritual nourishment for his or her soul. It was a thin place where the physical and spiritual intersected.

There are things associated with communion that current members of the Stone-Campbell movement may want to reconsider or explore more thoroughly. The practice of providing the Lord's Supper on Sunday evening looks more like a formal legality in some congregations rather than a meaningful moment of communion with the God of the Universe. It may also be helpful to recognize that all religious groups have liturgies. Some liturgies are informal or oral, but they are liturgies none the less. Acknowledging this and owning it could result in creating meaningful liturgies while also allowing space for extemporaneous prayers and devotional thoughts. Still, those within the Stone-Campbell movement have a beautiful history of worship involving the Lord's Supper, and I suspect most congregations are more than willing to deepen their understanding of the Lord's Supper while also making the practice more meaningful.

It is intriguing that when you read some of the beliefs of the early writers and thinkers of the Stone-Campbell movement regarding the Lord's Supper, they did not always clearly define every detail. For instance, many of them spoke of God's presence during the Lord's Supper or worship, but where was his presence located? Was it in the elements? Was it in the room? Was he seated at the table? Many of the writers were vague on this aspect and others, and one has to wonder if this was not on purpose. The Bible never defines this so why should they? If this is the case, then these men had something in common with a famous Christian writer that would come after them that would also try and unite Christians around the core beliefs of Christianity and the Lord's table. In commenting on the great divide among Christians regarding the Lord's Supper, C. S. Lewis reminds Christians, just as Campbell, Stone, and others did, that it is important to unite around what the Bible says rather than divide over what it does not say.

> I don't know and can't imagine what the disciples understood our Lord to mean when, His body still unbroken and His blood unshed, He handed them the bread and wine, saying they were His body and blood…I find 'substance' (in Aristotle's sense), when stripped of its own accidents and endowed with the accidents of some other substance, an object I cannot think…On the other hand, I get no better with those who tell me that the elements are mere bread and mere wine, used symbolically to remind me of the death of Christ. They are, on the natural level, such a very odd symbol of that…and I cannot see why this particular reminder – a hundred other things may, psychologically, remind me of Christ's death, equally, or perhaps more – should be so uniquely important as all Christendom (and my own heart) unhesitatingly declare…Yet I find no difficulty in believing that the veil between the worlds, nowhere else (for me) so opaque to the intellect, is nowhere else so thin and permeable to divine operation. Here a hand from the hidden country touches not only my soul but my body. Here the prig, the don, the modern, in me have no privilege over the savage or the child. Here is big medicine and strong

magic…the command, after all, was Take, eat: not Take, understand.[31]

Every Sunday in Churches of Christ around the world, the Lord's Supper is the focal point of worship. This is not a new trend. It was promoted by men like Campbell, Stone, Milligan, Richardson, and others who point to the centrality of the Lord's Supper among the early church. Congregations with ties to the Stone-Campbell movement have a rich tradition and theology of the Lord's Supper. This is not something that should be abandoned. It is a reason to stay and continue the work of striving to unite Christians around the table of our Lord.

> The glory that you have given me I have given to them, that they may be one even as we are one, I in them and you in me, that they may become perfectly one, so that the world may know that you sent me and loved them even as you loved me. (John 17:22-23)

---

[31] C. S. Lewis, *Letters to Malcolm*, p. 102-03.

I Stayed for the Singing

Benjamin J. Williams[1]

Introduction

I hope that the theological center of the Church of Christ is present in its name—Christ himself. However, it would be naïve to think this feature is our most distinguishing mark. For better or worse and often worse, the Church of Christ in the last century has been better known for worship wars — disputes over mode and style of worship — than for the proclamation of the gospel. Ask a stranger about us, and you will get the same first response: "You are the people who don't use instruments," instead of, "You are the people that embody the redeeming person and work of Jesus."

On the one hand, it is no surprise that a people's most unique practice would distinguish it, in the same way we might think of Roman Catholics as the people who have the pope. It is also no surprise that worship matters to us. Any group of people who get together once a week and share a sacred activity are going to care about that practice a great deal. I believe and hope to set forward in this text that this concern, though often misguided, is one of our

---

[1] Benjamin J. Williams is the Pulpit Minister for the Glenpool Church of Christ in Oklahoma. He holds a Bachelor of Science in Astrophysics from the University of Oklahoma and a Master of Divinity from Oklahoma Christian University. He has recently begun his work on a Ph.D. in Philosophy from Midwestern Baptist Theological Seminary. Along with Grant Sullivan, he cohosts a weekly sermon preparation podcast called Low Church Lectionarians, and he blogs at www.benpreachin.com. He and his wife, Selene, have two sons, Lucas and Calvin.

redeeming qualities. In particular, our commitment to a capella singing in worship is praiseworthy and theologically meaningful, if not for the reasons we might suspect.

The shocker for many frustrated members, ministers, and academics is what parts of our worship we choose to care about and the sharpness of our speech on this topic. In particular and above all else, the Church of Christ has sustained an intense conviction about instrumental music and its non-use. Most of our members do not know the Apostle's Creed, but we can give you detailed information about *psallo*. Wrapped in this issue is all that makes the Church of Christ good and fair, and also all that makes us less than we could be at this present hour.

The Basic Shape of the Instrumental Music Argument

While no definitive figure can speak for the "official" argument of the Church of Christ, Batsell Barrett Baxter summarizes the basic shape of the argument as follows:

> As a result of the distinctive plea of the church—a return to New Testament faith and practice—a cappella singing is the only music used in the worship. This singing, unaccompanied by mechanical [or electronic] instruments of music, conforms to the music used in the apostolic church and for several centuries thereafter (Ephesians 5:19). It is felt that there is no authority for engaging in acts of worship not found in the New Testament. This principle eliminates the use of instrumental music, along with the use of candles, incense, and other similar elements.[2]

Several lines of thought are represented here that should be considered individually.

---

[2] Batsell Barrett Baxter, "What Is the Church of Christ?" – a pamphlet based on a sermon Baxter preached at the Hillsboro Church of Christ in Nashville, January 23, 1955.

The argument the Church of Christ has advanced for many years is commonly called an argument from silence.[3] The idea is that (1) the church is guided and governed by the New Testament, but (2) the New Testament does not explicitly give reference to churches making use of instruments in their worship. Thus, it is concluded that by omitting the practice, the silence of Scriptures prohibits their use.

In response, some have challenged the first concept, that the church is governed and/or guided by the New Testament alone. A substantial case can be mounted from the Old Testament Scriptures that instruments were a part of Israel's worship. One need only read through the psalms to notice this is true. The typical counter to this suggestion is that the Old Testament is not the proper guide for Christian worship, as it also would authorize such practices as animal sacrifice, burning of incense, and regulations pertaining to the proper trimming of hair. The Christian, in rejecting some of those elements of Hebrew worship, would need to offer a criteria distinguishing between rules they wish to bind and rules they wish to ignore. James would find this difficult, "For whoever keeps the whole law but fails in one point has become accountable for all of it" (James 2:10).

Another response has been to find credible evidence of instrumental music in the New Testament. A scant few passages have been suggested, mainly instrumental references in the book of Revelation. However, Revelation with all its apocalyptic mystery is hardly a basic guide for Christian worship, and so is quite often dismissed. Furthermore, others have tried to make linguistic arguments about the word *psallo* found in the New Testament text and the possibility of instruments under the umbrella of that term (Ephesians 5:19). However, the linguistic evidence is shallow at best. The modern Greek language still uses the word *psaltes* for a chanter, and some lexicons acknowledge that at the time of the first century, the term narrowed in meaning to reference primarily singing from that time forward.[4]

---

[3] This is part of a larger hermeneutic of Command, Example, and Necessary Inference (CENI) which would require its own chapter to consider.

[4] Thayer and Smith. "Greek Lexicon entry for Psallo." Biblestudytools.com

Finally, a simpler response perhaps more common is to say that Scripture does not prohibit instruments and therefore allows them. In this, the Church of Christ falls back on its philosophical roots in Ulrich Zwingli and his arguments about authority with the Lutherans. For Zwingli and his fellow Swiss reformers, the church must only practice what is specifically authorized in Scripture.[5] Otherwise, it is argued, the door is now opened for adding virtually any absurd practice to our worship that is not expressly prohibited (soda for communion is a favorite example).

The grand finale of this argument is the conclusion that the inclusion of instruments in worship is an unauthorized innovation on the divine pattern of the New Testament. Those who worship without instruments are said to be standing squarely on divine authority. Those who worship with instruments are guilty of the sin of going beyond the boundaries of Christ's will and are therefore outside of the fellowship of God's people.

The Shortcomings of the Basic Argument

This basic line of argumentation has been hashed and rehashed for over a century. However, the basic argument has several built-in faults that need to be exposed and reformed. First, it relies on a very specific method of reading Scripture. If the New Testament is more descriptive than prescriptive, then God did not intend to list every possible activity his people might engage in any more than he sought to expressly prohibit every evil that humanity might imagine. The New Testament is the description of the normative practice of God's people, but it is not a list of precise details. This objection has been recognized more clearly in the "anti-" wing of the Church of Christ, the group that excludes Sunday Schools and/or support of certain children's homes based on Biblical silence in the same way that the mainline Church of Christ excludes instruments.[6] In order to continue reading the New Testament prescriptively, one must continually make hair-splitting decisions

---

[5] C. Leonard Allen and Richard T. Hughes, *Discovering Our Roots: The Ancestry of Churches of Christ* (Abilene, TX: ACU Press, 1988), 21-33.

[6] I apologize that the term "anti-" may be read pejoratively. Such is not my intent here.

about what is permitted or excluded by Biblical silence, what is expedient and what is not.

The greater shortcoming of the basic argument is seen in how it is practiced on the congregational level. The argument from silence leads to a self-contradictory practice. It leads to ministers preaching sermons about a topic they willingly admit is not in the Scriptures. If the goal is to be silent where the Bible is silent, then the minister must be silent on the topic of instrumental music. Yet, a survey of the books, sermons, and articles published by the Church of Christ quickly makes it clear that we have not been silent on this topic. Ironically, we have been extremely vocal in regards to an issue that is absent from Scripture, and our main point is that we should be silent about topics which are absent from Scripture.

Another way to express this concern is to search the Scriptures for any passage that gives any consideration to this topic. Why in the exhaustive array of topics considered by Paul in his epistles — from circumcision to the appropriate attire of women — does the topic of appropriate worship music not come up? More importantly, why do I feel motivated to preach on a subject the Holy Spirit never bothered with in twenty-seven books of the New Testament? Our argument from silence should be our undoing. We should be more silent, and speak as the oracles of God.

Instead of honoring silence, we have spoken into God's silence, and in our frequent protests, we have alienated fellow believers over a topic never mentioned in the only book that can ever be the safe rule for faith and practice. All of this is done while persisting the New Testament doesn't mention it. The irony is actually painful.

Furthermore, we — the people who claim to reject all creeds and human opinions — have replaced these influences with a very specific kind of human reasoning. We would do well to remember the premise stated by Thomas Campbell in "Declaration and Address":

> That although inferences and deductions from Scripture premises, when fairly inferred, may be truly called the doctrine of God's holy word, yet are they not formally binding upon the consciences of Christians farther than they perceive the connection, and evidently see that they are so; for their faith must not stand in the wisdom of men, but in the power and

veracity of God. Therefore, no such deductions can be made terms of communion, but do properly belong to the after and progressive edification of the Church. Hence, it is evident that no such deductions or inferential truths ought to have any place in the Church's confession.[7]

The Surprising Strengths of the Practice

Having said all that, I still believe strongly in a capella worship. The Church of Christ has maintained a very healthy and formative worship practice, though probably for some misguided reasons.

Canon & Tradition

First, a capella worship does fit the description of Christian worship given in Scripture and early church history. We do not have to be advocates of a negative or prescriptive doctrine to notice instruments just do not come up much in our New Testaments. The early church seems to have arrived at the same conclusion, for differing reasons, that instruments were not part of Christian worship. In this, the Church of Christ — almost by accident — finds itself in wholesome agreement with two millennia of church history and practice.[8] The argument from silence was never found in ancient Christianity, but the practice of singing without instruments is found and often defended. From the church fathers to the Reformation, the practice of singing without instruments in the chapel has been normal. The practice of the Church of Christ is not an outlier; only our intensity in condemning the opposing view

---

[7] Thomas Campbell, "Declaration and Address," 1809.

[8] The definitive work on this topic is Everett Ferguson, *A Cappella Music In the Public Worship of the Church* (Abilene, TX: Desert Willow Publishing, 2013). To engage the larger conversation, read the opposite position expressed in Danny Corbitt, *Missing More Than Music: When Disputable Matters Eclipse Worship and Unity* (Bloomington: AuthorHouse, 2008). Finally, see Ferguson's response to Corbitt, in Everett Ferguson, "Missing the Meaning: A Review of *Missing More Than Music*," *Gospel Advocate* (September 2010): 33-35. As another recent resource challenging this conclusion, see David John Shirt, "'Sing to the Lord with the harp': Attitudes to musical instruments in early Christianity, 680 A.D." (PhD diss., Durham University, 2015).

and our particular way of reasoning to that conclusion is abnormal in Christian history.

The Regulatory Principle

Second, whatever the weakness of our hermeneutic, it does have roots in the regulatory principle voiced so strongly in the Reformation.[9] Calvin states it repeatedly in *The Necessity of Reforming the Church*.

> Therefore, if we would have him to approve our worship, this rule, which he everywhere enforces with the utmost strictness, must be carefully observed. For there is a twofold reason why the Lord, in condemning and prohibiting all fictitious worship, requires us to give obedience only to his own voice. First, it tends greatly to establish his authority that we do not follow our own pleasure, but depend entirely on his sovereignty; and, secondly, such is our folly, that when we are left at liberty, all we are able to do is to go astray. And then when once we have turned aside from the right path, there is no end to our wanderings, until we get buried under a multitude of superstitions. Justly, therefore, does the Lord, in order to assert his full right of dominion, strictly enjoin what he wishes us to do, and at once reject all human devices which are at variance with his command. Justly, too, does he, in express terms, define our limits, that we may not, by fabricating perverse modes of worship, provoke his anger against us.[10]

A similar statement may be found in the *Baptist Confession of Faith* of 1689:

> [God] is to be feared, loved, praised, called upon, trusted in, and served, with all the heart and all the soul, and with all the might. But the acceptable way of worshipping the true God has been instituted by Himself, and therefore our method of

---

[9] A good look at its influence on the Westminster Confession is John Allen Delivuk, "Biblical Authority and the Proof of the Regulative Principle of Worship in The Westminster Confession," *The Westminster Theological Journal* 58, no. 2 (September 1996): 237-256.

[10] Calvin, *The Necessity of Reforming the Church*, 1543.

worship is limited by His own revealed will. He may not be worshipped according to the imagination and devices of men, nor the suggestions of Satan. He may not be worshipped by way of visible representations, or by any other way not prescribed in the Holy Scriptures.[11]

What is contained in each of these highly contested statements is the important reformed concept that the canon is the guide for Christian worship. While Calvin, the Baptists, the Puritans, and the Restoration Movement among many others have all wrestled with the application of this principle, none deny its efficacy. That it must exist in some form is an implication produced from two important Reformation doctrines.

First, the regulative principle as applied to worship is a derivative of the broader concept of *sola scriptura*. The principle affirms the language of the Scriptures as normative, and this conclusion has been essential to Christianity in some form for its entire history. Canon exists for the very purpose of being a normative rule. Karl Barth states the function of canon as follows:

> Theology has…its position *beneath* that of the biblical scriptures. While it is aware of all their human and conditioned character, it still knows and considers that the writings with which it deals are *holy* writings. These writing are selected and separated; they deserve and demand respect and attention of an extraordinary order, since they have a direct relationship to God's work and word. … The biblical witnesses are better informed than are the theologians. For this reason theology must agree to let *them* look over its shoulder and correct its notebooks.[12]

Miroslav Volf would agree with this identification of theology and theological activity as an echo of Canon: "In my judgment, Scripture is an indispensable and critical source of theological reflection because it is the primary site of God's self-revelation."[13] He calls

---

[11] Baptist Confession of Faith of 1689, 22.1.

[12] Karl Barth, *Evangelical Theology: An Introduction* (Grand Rapids, MI: Eerdmans, 1979), 32.

[13] Miroslav Volf, *Captive to the Word of God: Engaging the Scriptures for Contemporary Theological Reflection* (Grand Rapids, MI: Eerdmans, 2010), 6.

the Bible "the document that lies at the heart of the life of Christian communities, the texts on which these communities depend for existence, identity, and vitality."[14] Without the Bible, Volf will go on to state,

> The result will be a culturally and socially barren theology that hovers above concrete communities of faith – or maybe falls to the ground beside them – unable to shape either these communities or the wider culture.

Scripture is, in the words of Luke Timothy Johnson,

> [T]he church's working bibliography...Whatever else is read and studied in private, these writings are used by the assembly as such for debating and defining its identity.[15]

If Scripture is the normative rule for Christian practice, then, of course, it must be considered as a primary source for the consideration of Christian worship, the church's most radical and formative act.

Furthermore, the regulative principle and its cousins are tied to the doctrine of the sovereignty of God.[16] As Calvin explains above, if all creation is subject to God, then surely creation's worship must also be so subject. To be subject is to act by first asking. Subjection to God's sovereignty means God's self-revelation is primary and every other concern secondary. In pursuing worship from the launching point of God's revealed desire rather than humanity's current mood, we are at least having the right argument, though we do not often have it well. Humanity is a reflector of God's glory, not its originator. If our worship is to be theologically sound, it must begin with God's self-revelation in Christ Jesus and the Scriptures as His continued voice in the community of faith. How do our Scriptures shape every part of our worship? This question must continue to be asked, debated, and explored in our churches.

---

[14] Ibid., 11-12.

[15] Luke Timothy Johnson, *Scripture & Discernment: Decision-Making in the Church* (Nashville: Abingdon Press, 1996), 35.

[16] I am personally not married to the word "sovereignty" due to the embellishments sometimes put onto this term by Protestants, but it serves a purpose here. In other discussions, a better term might be suitable.

Consumer Driven Worship

Third, by following the historic precedent and a form of the regulative principle, we avoid one of the frustrating scandals of modern worship, the diminishing voice of the collective church in favor of the performance of a select group. Many prominent evangelical pastors have spoken out with concerns that modern worship has increasingly turned the formative worship described in the Scriptures into a spectator sport. They have wondered aloud how to reclaim their devotion from "worshiptainment."[17] John Piper wrote:

> Thirteen years ago we asked: What should be the defining sound of corporate worship at Bethlehem [Piper's home congregation], besides the voice of biblical preaching? We meant: Should it be pipe organ, piano, guitar, drums, choir, worship team, orchestra, etc. The answer we gave was 'The people of Bethlehem singing.' Some thought: That's not much help in deciding which instruments should be used. Perhaps not. But it is massively helpful in clarifying the meaning of those moments. If Bethlehem is not 'singing and making melody to the Lord with [our] heart,' (Ephesians 5:19), it's all over. We close up shop. This is no small commitment.[18]

Piper is not stating opposition to instruments, only a concern that the modern praise band has diminished the voice of the church. Likewise, James K. A. Smith, Professor of Philosophy at Calvin College and Editor of *Comment* magazine, writes the following three points about our worship through music:

1. If we, the congregation, can't hear ourselves, it's not worship.

2. If we, the congregation, can't sing along, it's not worship.

---

[17] Mike Livingstone, "The Heresy of Worshiptainment," mikelivingston.com. January 12, 2015. Accessed 1/21/15. Also, Bob Kauflin, "How Do We Move Away from 'Worshiptainment'?" worshipmatters.com. May 12, 2006. Accessed 1/21/15.

[18] John Piper, "The Importance of Corporate Singing," desiringgod.com. September 4, 2008. Accessed 1/21/15.

3. If you, the praise band, are the center of attention, it's not worship.[19]

Singing shapes our worship, and worship shapes our ecclesial identity. In much the same way sharing a loaf and a cup make us one body (1 Cor 10:16-17), partaking of one song with one voice shapes our identity in Christ.

Here, the Church of Christ bears witness to a powerful alternative to consumer-driven worship, the simple and formative singing of the church. This is not to say a capella singing cannot be consumer driven and superficial, but it does offer an avenue of worship which has the capacity to more often avoid these pitfalls. Sadly, few are listening to what the Church of Christ has offered, because we have framed too much of the debate in terms which are doomed to failure and ultimately to irrelevance. By condemning a behavior louder than we modeled a positive alternative, we have muted ourselves in a world that needs our voice. It does not have to be so.

The Way Forward

I believe a capella singing remains a bright part of the future of the Church of Christ. The convictions represented in our worship are worthwhile, and yes, they are one of the many reasons I will be sticking around in our fellowship. The way forward is to maintain our conviction without condescension. We have something good in a capella music. It is a form of worship that simultaneously conforms to the New Testament description, repeats the voice of church history, and speaks out against the consumer-driven spectator worship that too often characterizes our times. I repeat, we have something good. We should maintain it, but not as a prescription or as a small marked box on a divine checklist. We must never forget our own point, that the Scriptures are silent on this issue. Our rebuke of instrumental music in worship must never be louder than that of the New Testament. Our opposition to one believer's worship must not be louder than our magnification of He who is

---

[19] Excerpts from James K. A. Smith, "An Open Letter to Praise Bands," forsclavigera.blogspot.com. February 20, 2012. Accessed 1/21/15.

to be worshipped. In this, we can truly live up to our name and be a church of Christ, not a church of contention.

God, let it be so.

I Stayed for the Wild Democracy

John Mark Hicks[1]

Between 1880 and 1920 two identities emerged within the American Restoration Movement. One tended to utilize the name "Christian Church" on its sign while others used the designation "Church of Christ." In 1903, James A. Harding lamented congregations have divided in "hundreds of places all over our land" over the past "forty-three years" such that in "the same city, town or village we find the 'Church of Christ' and the 'Christian Church,' the two having no Christian fellowship for each other."[2] This formal distinction is evidenced by A. M. Morris's 1891 pamphlet entitled *Difference Between the Church of Christ and the Christian Church*.[3]

Many factors contributed to this division. Some are sociological (including North-South sectionalism, urban/rural demographics, rich/poor economics) and some are theological. The

---

[1] John Mark Hicks has taught theology and history courses at Lipscomb University since 2000. He received his B.A. in Bible from Freed-Hardeman University (1977), his M.A.R. in Theological Studies from Westminster Theological Seminary (1980), his M.A. in Humanities from Western Kentucky University (1981) and his Ph.D. in Reformation and Post-Reformation Studies from Westminster Theological Seminary (1985). He has taught theology since 1982, including nine years at Harding University Graduate School of Religion (1991-2000). He has ministered with churches in Virginia, Pennsylvania, Alabama, and Tennessee. He has published nine books and thirteen journal articles as well as contributed to nineteen other books. He has spoken in thirty-eight states and nineteen countries. He and his wife, Jennifer, have five living children and two deceased.

[2] James A. Harding, "Our Practice," *The Way* 5 (13 August 1903) 786.

[3] A. M. Morris, *Difference Between the Church of Christ and the Christian Church* (Moberly, MO: Sentinel Printing Co., 1891).

rise of ecumenism, biblical higher criticism, and female pastors among some Christian Churches were the most significant theological factors, more decisive than instrumental music and missionary societies. Symbolically, the division is dated from 1906 because David Lipscomb told the Census Office the two groups were "separate and distinct in name, work, and rule of faith."[4] The 1906 Census formally acknowledged the split, and churches of Christ represented only 14% (159,658 members), and 60% of those lived in Texas, Tennessee, and Arkansas (only 10% lived north of the Ohio and east of the Mississippi rivers).

As churches of Christ emerged as a "new religious movement" from the 1880s to 1930s, David Harrell notes, they practiced a "wild democracy" where they sought consensus by engaging in free and open discussions without the entanglements of creedalism, traditionalism, and institutionalism. Between 1906 and 1926 the churches of Christ were "just beginning to define [their] own identity."[5] This identity was "gathered, clarified and explained," according to William Woodson, in the N. B. Hardeman Nashville revivals conducted in 1921, 1923, 1928, 1938, and 1942.[6] Hardeman described these meetings as telling "Nashville, as nothing else could have, who we were."[7]

That identity was solidified through urban meetings, prominent literature (such as C. R. Nichols and Robert L. Whiteside's five-volume *Sound Doctrine* and established journals like the *Firm Foundation* and *Gospel Advocate*), and college lectureships (Abilene Christian College and Freed-Hardeman College). From the 1880s through the 1930s, churches of Christ discussed their identity, and in the 1940s a general uniformity was realized with only some marginal dissent (e.g., Harding College did not always follow the con-

---

[4] David Lipscomb, "The 'Church of Christ' and the 'Disciples of Christ'," *Gospel Advocate* 49 (18 July 1907) 450. The *Gospel Advocate* is hereafter abbreviated as *GA*.

[5] David Edwin Harrell, *The Churches of Christ in the Twentieth Century: Homer Hailey's Personal Journey of Faith* (Tuscaloosa: University of Alabama Press, 2000) 9, 40, 42.

[6] William Woodson, *Standing for Their Faith: A History of the Churches of Christ in Tennessee, 1900-1950)* (Henderson, TN: J & W Publications, 1979) 74-75.

[7] N. B. Hardeman, *Hardeman's Tabernacle Sermons, IV* (Nashville: Gospel Advocate, 1938) 9.

sensus). Though a further split developed in the 1950s over institutionalism, there was nevertheless general uniformity about the identity of churches of Christ as an ecclesial reality. By the mid-1940s, the "wild democracy" had essentially run its course. The 1960s, however, challenged this uniformity as a "wild democracy" re-emerged, though strongly and vigorously opposed by the 1950s uniformity, and many lost standing in the community because they challenged that uniformity.

The disagreements within this early 20th-century "wild democracy" were significant. Theological differences among churches of Christ, for example, ranged from polity issues (e.g., number, qualification, selection, ordination, and authority of elders) to materialism (e.g., soul-sleep), from mutual edification to located evangelists, from the corporate practice of the right hand of fellowship to the necessity of confession before baptism, from a prescribed order of worship to legitimate uses of the contribution on Sunday, from women working outside the home to female participation in the assembly, from involvement in politics to institutionalism (including Sunday Schools and Bible colleges), from debating the relation of the kingdom to the church to whether the Sermon on the Mount applies to Christians, from war-peace questions to social involvement in temperance movements, from the nature of special providence to the reality of contemporary miracles, and from biblical names for the church to eschatology (millennialism as well as renewed earth theology).[8]

Since it is impossible to cover all these differences, I have chosen to illustrate this "wild democracy" by highlighting three disagreements; each were hotly debated and threatened to split churches of Christ. These are rebaptism, the female voice in the assembly, and the indwelling of the Holy Spirit.

---

[8] This paragraph and some material in this chapter are adapted from my "The Struggle for the Soul of Churches of Christ (1897-1907): Hoosiers, Volunteers, and Longhorns," 54-71, in *And the WORD became Flesh: Studies in History, Communication and Scripture in Memory of Michael W. Casey*, ed. Thomas H. Olbricht and David Fleer (Eugene, OR: Pickwick Publications, 2009).

Rebaptism

Over two hundred articles were exchanged on the subject of rebaptism from 1897 to 1907. Harding debated the question with both Austin McGary and J. D. Tant; T. R. Burnett debated McGary; and J. C. McQuiddy debated John S. Durst. Lipscomb and McGary exchanged numerous articles in the *Firm Foundation* (hereafter *FF*) and *GA*. Tant, however, expected within "fifteen years" people "coming into the fellowship of the church of Christ on their sectarian baptism [would] be a thing of the past" because "the *gospel* is having its leavening influence in Tennessee."[9] He was essentially correct, though it took a bit longer. In 1957, Fanning Yater Tant—J.D.'s son—claimed the *FF* "saved the day in that battle" through "free, open, and unfettered discussion of the issue" as the "church was finally brought to a general agreement," though it was by no means unanimous.[10] Ironically, Fanning asked for a "free, open, and unfettered" discussion of institutionalism, which was then dividing the church. B. C. Goodpasture, editor of the *GA*, enforced uniformity through a kind of quarantine practice.[11]

The specific question was whether Baptists (or other immersed believers) should be re-immersed in order to receive the "right hand of fellowship" for entrance into a congregation of the Church of Christ. For Lipscomb, Harding, and Daniel Sommer, anyone immersed upon a confession of faith in Jesus as the Messiah, the Son of God, is a Christian. For McGary and Tant, only those immersed with the specific knowledge their baptism was the moment of salvation are Christians.

This was a *gospel* issue for the *FF*. McGary, for example, believed the *GA* was "going beyond the authority of the Lord" on the basic question of who is a Christian. This was more liberal, damaging and insidious than the society and the organ, and it

---

[9] J. D. Tant, "Too Many Papers," *FF* 15 (10 January 1899) 23 (emphasis mine).

[10] Fanning Yater Tant, "Pride, Prejudice, and Papers," *Gospel Guardian* 9.11 (18 July 1957) 4.

[11] Cf. John C. Hardin, "Common Cause: B. C. Goodpasture, the *Gospel Advocate*, and Churches of Christ in the Twentieth Century" (Ph.D. dissertation, Auburn University, 2009) 154.

would ultimately lead to a "divided brotherhood."¹² It is a *gospel* issue because the *GA* receives as Christians those who are not authentically Christian. This is the real "rub" for the *FF*. It expanded the borders of the kingdom beyond those identified with churches of Christ who baptize explicitly "for the remission of sins." At root, the *GA* "was teaching other ways that sinners may be forgiven and enter the kingdom of Christ."¹³ It was "shaking in the Baptists" by extending the "right hand of fellowship" to Baptists who seek to unite with a congregation. By so doing, they acknowledge Christians among the sects, and this embraced a broader vision of the kingdom than was comfortable for the *FF*. G. W. Savage, the editor of the *FF*, wrote that his paper "has never 'fallen' so far as to teach this conglomeration of faithless 'union' and communion."¹⁴

The *GA* saw the "rub" differently. Lipscomb stressed that obedience to Jesus through faith was a sufficient motive for effective baptism.¹⁵ To require more is to undermine simple obedience since not faith but knowledge and doctrinal precision determine acceptable obedience. When faith in Jesus moves one to obedience, that is sufficient no matter what else one knows or does not know or even falsely believes about their baptism. It is faith in the work of God rather than faith in the human understanding of baptismal design. Consequently, as Harding argued,"[t]hough [someone] may have a thousand false notions, and scarcely understands one other doctrine of the Bible, [the one seeking baptism] has one right: he

---

[12] McGary, "The Firm Foundation—Its Aims and Principles," *FF* 16 (8 January 1901) 8. McGary, "Editorial," *FF* 14 (13 September 1898) 284: "But the trouble between us is traceable to the very same presumptuous spirit that brings the society and the organ into the work and worship of the church. Bros. Lipscomb, Harding and their wicked confederates in this attack upon us claim to speak where the Bible speaks and to be silent where the Bible is silent."

[13] McGary, "Aims and Principles," 8.

[14] George W. Savage, "Brother Burnett's Charges," *FF* 21 (28 November 1905) 4.

[15] David Lipscomb, "What Constitutes Acceptable Obedience?" in *Salvation from Sin*, ed. J. W. Shepherd (Nashville, TN: Gospel Advocate Co., 1913) 208-234.

does believe with his whole heart that Jesus is the Christ, the Son of the living God; and this is perfect preparation for baptism."[16]

Daniel Sommer, as well as Lipscomb and Harding, believed the *FF* position was itself sectarian because it excludes those whom God includes. "The rebaptism extreme, as advocated by many, is an intensely sectarian idea."[17] In 1891 Sommer published a tract defending the validity of any baptism performed "in the name of the Godhead" to a penitent who confessed Jesus as the Son of God. He thought it important to publish it because the *FF* was intent on "working division in the brotherhood."[18]

The rebaptism controversy was a struggle within churches of Christ about the borders of the kingdom of God. It signaled a move toward a more pronounced exclusivism. While the *GA* perspective lost this struggle (even within the pages of the *GA* from the 1930s to the present), it did not die but remained alive in various places among churches of Christ (e.g., Harding College).[19] In the 1960s, and particularly in the 1980s, it once again became a topic within the "wild democracy."

Feminine Voice in the Assembly[20]

One of the forgotten debates from the first decades of the 20th century among churches of Christ is whether audible participation in the assembly through prayer, singing, and exhortation was a woman's "privilege" or a subversion of the created order. This was a live issue at the turn of the 20th century even though it was not resurrected again until near the beginning of the 21st century. It created considerable anxiety. After years of discussion, Charles

---

[16] Harding, "The Faith That Prepares for Baptism," *CLW* 18 (1 November 1904) 9.

[17] As quoted by N. L. Clark, "On the Firing Line," *FF* 22 (6 November 1906) 4. Cf. Daniel Sommer, "Items of Interest," *Octographic Review* 40 (23 March 1897) 1. Hereafter cited as *OR*.

[18] Sommer, "Let Patience Have Her Perfect Work," *OR* 40 (29 June 1897) 1, 8.

[19] Cf. Jimmy Allen, *Rebaptism: What One Must Know to be Born Again* (Monroe: Howard Books, 1991).

[20] This is adapted from my "Quiet Please: Churches of Christ in the Early Twentieth Century and the 'Woman Question'," *Discipliana* 68.2 (Fall 2009) 7-24.

Black lamented the disagreement. "When I read these differences by brethren who seemingly are wise in other things," he wrote, "it makes me glad that I am not a woman."[21]

Though most everyone within churches of Christ thought female pastors were outside the biblical norm, there were diverse answers to the questions whether a female voice might lead the public assembly in singing, prayer, Scripture reading, and exhortation/edification. In general, while the *GA* and *FF* (though with some dissent) answered the question in the negative, the *Octographic Review* and many writers in the *Christian Leader* (hereafter *CL*) answered affirmatively.

The editors of the *GA* grounded their conclusion in a broad understanding of the role of women in society as dictated by the order of creation. They believed women were forbidden any kind of *public* leadership whether in church or society. Consequently, not only are they excluded from speaking in the worshipping assembly, they should not speak publicly anywhere. Not only are they excluded from functioning as elders in the church, but they also should not become business leaders, presidents, or school teachers. Elisha G. Sewell, for example, based on Genesis 3:16, believed "woman...has never been put forward as a leader among men in *any public capacity* from the garden of Eden till now." [22] Lipscomb and Harding shared this conviction, and one of their more prominent students, R. C. Bell, illustrates its depth. "Woman," he writes, "is not permitted to exercise dominion over man in *any calling of life*. When a woman gets her diploma to practice medicine, every Bible student knows that she is violating God's holy law." This principle excludes her not only from the "pulpit," but also from practicing law or "the public school room." "When God gives his reason for woman's subjection and quietness," he continues, "he covers the whole ground and forbids her to work *in any public capacity*." [23]

These are strong words, and they are so distant from our contemporary context we might cringe when reading them. Yet, one

---

[21] Charles S. Black, "That Awful Woman Question?" *Christian Leader & the Way* 21 (19 November 1907) 4.

[22] Elisha G. Sewell, "What is Woman's Work in the Church (Again)?" *GA* 39 (22 July 1897) 432 (emphasis mine).

[23] R. C. Bell, "Woman's Work," *The Way* 5 (6 August 1903) 775.

may admire the consistency. "That man should rule is the ordinance of God that grows out of the natures" of men and women. "God put in him the ruling qualities," according to Harding. While women are "very much superior to men" in many ways, "her superiority is not in leadership."[24]

Since, in this perspective, women were inferior to men in leadership capacity and excluded from any "public" life, it is not surprising to see the New Testament construed in a way that fits this presupposition. When seeking to inductively collect and harmonize the New Testament's teaching on "woman's work," many concluded the most significant distinction was public versus private. Women "must pray and teach, but not publicly."[25]

Priscilla taught Apollos along with Aquilla. Phillip's daughters prophesied. Corinthian women prayed and prophesied. "Women announced the resurrection to the eleven" and the Samaritan woman "proclaimed" Jesus "as the Christ to the people of her city." "The fact that," Harding continued, "women in the apostolic age prophesied (spoke by inspiration) makes it clear to my mind that women who know God's Word now should teach it." But this "by no means necessarily implies that she taught in the public meetings of the church."[26]

The discerning principle is not whether a woman may teach or not teach, or pray or not pray. Rather, it is the sphere in which she teaches or prays, and the context determines the nature of the leadership involved. "[T]heir spheres are different."[27] Her sphere is the home rather than the "great assembly." Since God created man as "the leader, the ruler," when a woman "assumes the leadership" through prayer or teaching in the public sphere as she "directs and controls" the "thoughts" of others she then "takes a place for which she was not made."[28] That sphere belongs to men whereas women were given "the humbler, better place and more difficult

---

[24] Harding, "Woman's Work in the Church," *Christian Leader & the Way* 18 (8 March 1904) 9.

[25] Bell, "Woman's Work," *The Way* 5 (3 December 1903) 1046 (emphasis mine).

[26] Harding, "Woman's Work," 8.

[27] O. A. Carr, "Woman's Work in the Church, What She Should Do in Public Worship. No. 3," *Christian Leader & the Way* 19 (30 May 1905) 1.

[28] Harding, "Woman's Work," 8.

work," that is, the domestic life.[29] "Her place," Poe wrote, "is at home to guide the house [and] rear the children."[30] This principle is rooted in Creation and illustrated by the Fall. Eve "wrecked things when she took the leadership in Eden."[31] Succinctly, according to Bell, a woman "can teach anybody anywhere except in cases where *publicity* is connected with it."[32]

This consensus among southern churches, in both Tennessee and Texas (though with some dissent), became a line in the sand just like instrumental music or baptism. "That women are not allowed to make speeches in the meetings of the churches," Harding noted, "is just as plainly and strongly taught as that believers are to be baptized."[33] When congregations permit women to "lead the prayers, to speak and to exhort in the meetings of the church," Harding thought, "God's law was" no more "flagrantly violated than...at this point."[34]

In January 1904, the *Christian Leader* and *The Way* merged. Though a friendly merger, it united Harding's southern paper with a northern paper whose roots were shared by Daniel Sommer. This entailed some substantial differences (e.g., pacifism, institutionalism, special providence), including the "woman question." The *Christian Leader* had a significant history of openness toward female participation in the assembly through prayer, Scripture reading, and exhortation. In 1897, for example, Ben Atkins offered "a Scriptural call for women to resume Christian activity in the church, praying, speaking, exhorting, singing, teaching, as in the apostolic age in Corinth."[35]

Consequently, when Harding staked out his ground on the "woman question" as co-editor of the new *Christian Leader & the Way* (hereafter *CLW*), he found himself in hot water with some

---

[29] Henry Hawley, "Woman and Her Work," *The Way* 5 (20 August 1903) 810.

[30] John T. Poe, "Female Evangelists," *FF* 16 (29 January 1901) 2.

[31] Harding, "Scraps," *The Way* 3 (20 March 1902) 393.

[32] Bell, "Woman's Work," 777 (emphasis mine).

[33] Harding, "Was Paul Mistaken, Or Did He Lie About It, or Are I Cor. 14:33-35 and I Tim. 2:8-13 Both True?" *CLW* 21 (26 November 1907) 8.

[34] Harding, "Brethren Faurott, Sands and the Woman Question," *Christian Leader & the Way* 21 (17 December 1907) 8.

[35] Ben Atkins, "The Woman Question," *CL* 11 (2 February 1897) 2.

readers. W. J. Brown of Cloverdale, Indiana, for example, cautioned "before we force upon the churches our narrow, ignorant interpretations of the Bible, we ought to go back and study the question again."[36] Also, F. U. Harmon tersely rebuked some writers: "Don't forbid these women, as you have been doing."[37] And Foster, letting Harding know northerners did things a bit different, wrote, "it is not counted immodest here, in these times, for a woman to speak or pray, even in the churches" and since "we find where they prophesied" in the New Testament, "why not now?"[38]

Daniel Sommer, the leader of what is often regarded as the right wing of churches of Christ at the turn of the century, shared this perspective. His article, "Woman's Religious Duties and Privileges in Public," summarizes his position.[39] "Extremes beget extremes," Sommer began. The extreme of female evangelists (pastors) had begat the extreme of silencing women in the assembly. It had now become a hobby for some writers. He suggested a middle ground practiced by churches in his long experience. It is a woman's privilege to "*publicly read* in audible tones a portion of Scripture" in the assembly. This included her "privilege to teach a class in a meeting house" since the class is not the publicly assembled congregation. Further, since exhortation and teaching are different, even during the assembly, "if a sister in good standing wishes to arise in a congregation and offer an exhortation it is her privilege to do so." A woman's privilege in the assembly, then, includes audible prayer, public reading of Scripture, public exhortation, and teaching a Bible class of men, women and/or children. Since the assembly is a "meeting of the family of God," where "there is neither male nor female," everyone—both male and female—should "admonish one another" as per Romans 15:14. When "the whole church is come together," women are authorized and encouraged "to speak to the edification, exhortation and comfort of the church."[40]

---

[36] W. J. Brown, "Notes of Passing Interest," *CLW* 18 (16 August 1904) 5.

[37] F. U. Harmon, "The Woman Question," *CLW* 18 (6 September 1904) 9.

[38] W. W. Foster, "Twelve Women and Two Men," *CLW* 18 (18 February 1904) 4.

[39] Sommer, "Woman's Religious Duties and Privileges in Public," *Octographic Review* 34 (20 August 1901) 1.

[40] W. D. Cameron, "Your Women," *Octographic Review* 48 (11 April 1905) 2.

Ultimately, the *GA* won the day, even though it moderated its views on women in society such that one hears little opposition to female doctors, lawyers, and CEOs today. In essence, and quite effectively, it silenced the female voice in the public assemblies of churches of Christ. The openness of Sommer-influenced congregations died out as southern churches of Christ overwhelmed them in number, influence, and institutional power. Sommer's position, though largely forgotten except by a few historians, was unwittingly renewed in some quarters of churches of Christ in the late 20th century, though it remains a minority *via media* between the traditional and egalitarian positions. In other words, the "wild democracy" has re-emerged in recent decades.

The Holy Spirit

Other than rebaptism, the work of the indwelling Spirit was the most controversial topic in the first decade of the 20th century. Over one hundred articles were exchanged on the topic in the years 1904-1906 alone. These involved some heated interactions such as the explosive discussion between J. C. Holloway and James A. Harding in the 1905 *CLW*.[41] When *The Way* and *CL* merged in 1904, Harding's strong belief in the enabling power of the indwelling Spirit was opposed by some elements of the *CL* constituency[42] and ultimately led J. S. Warlick, a leader in Texas, to begin the *Gospel Guide* where he endorsed Holloway.[43]

The Holloway-Harding exchanges, however, were anticipated in 1897-1898 when J. W. Denton of the *FF* and T. R. Burnett of the *GA*—who both joined the fray in 1905 as well—hammered out the question. Generally, the *OR* sat out these discussions because they thought it a settled question. Bittle, for example, occasionally answers questions regarding the issue as if there were no

---

[41] John Mark Hicks and Bobby Valentine, *Kingdom Come: Embracing the Spiritual Legacy of David Lipscomb and James Harding* (Abilene: Leafwood Press, 2006), 60-66.

[42] B. F. Bixler, "Another Voice," *CLW* 30 (18 July 1905) 2.

[43] Joe S. Warlick, "Let Your Women Keep Silent in the Churches," *Gospel Guide* 5 (August 1920) 2.

real dispute—it is, he wrote, "as most Christians allow."⁴⁴ "Indwelling personally with and in the saints," according to Bittle, "the Holy Spirit acts as the representative of Christ and God."⁴⁵ Sommer also dismisses attempts to reduce the presence of the Spirit to information or testimony. On the contrary, the testimony of the Spirit is that God gives "obedient believers" the Spirit "personally, entering their hearts and dwelling in them."⁴⁶

The *FF* stood firmly against any conception of the indwelling Spirit other than through the word alone.⁴⁷ The *FF* opposed the personal and enabling power of the Spirit as a form of "mysticism," an "absurd idea...purely sectarian in origin."⁴⁸ Advocates of such are still "in the fog of sectarian mysticism."⁴⁹ The subjective nature of the supposed comfort and help of the indwelling Spirit was, in the minds of many, analogous to the "mourner's bench" and "Pentecostial (*sic*) showers."⁵⁰ It rendered the word insufficient because the Spirit operates directly. If "the Spirit comes from God to the Christian, then" this is "direct operation" and if the "Spirit (as a person) dwells in the church today, then the days of miracles are not past and the Mormons are right."⁵¹ Instead, the word is sufficient as God "leads, guides, controls men by his Word" and he does not "have to be here personally to do it."⁵²

More specifically, Denton's position reduces to an empirical epistemology of language. God comforts by words because "you can not comfort anything that has no ideas, and you can not have ideas without words."⁵³ Since, according to Denton, humans can only be "influenced" by "coercion" and "moral suasion," the Spirit

---

⁴⁴ L. F. Bittle, "The Invocation of the Spirit," *OR* 40 (11 May 1897) 4.

⁴⁵ Bittle, "The Gift of the Holy Ghost," *OR* 44 (26 November 1901) 4.

⁴⁶ Sommer, "Concerning What the Holy Spirit Says to Sinner and Saints," *OR* 46 (14 July 1903), 1. Other examples are E. C. Richardson, "The Work of the Holy Spirit. Fourteenth Article. The Operation of the Spirit," *OR* 45 (4 May 1902) 2, and Henry Benge, "My Experience with the Doctrine of the In-Dwelling Holy Spirit," *OR* 48 (2 May 1905) 3.

⁴⁷ G. A. Trott, "The Indwelling Spirit," *FF* 22 (13 March 1906) 4.

⁴⁸ G. T. Walker, "The Indwelling of the Spirit," *FF* 15 (20 June 1899) 385.

⁴⁹ L. C. Chisholm, "Spiritual Influence," *FF* 21 (14 November 1905) 2.

⁵⁰ G. T. Walker, "The Indwelling of the Spirit," *FF* 15 (20 June 1899) 385.

⁵¹ J. W. Denton, "Reflections on the Spirit," *FF* 20 (9 February 1904) 1.

⁵² Denton, "Bro. Burnett's Muddle Again," *FF* 14 (6 September 1898) 282.

⁵³ J. Denton, "Muddle Again," 282.

does not act on the human heart, whether for sinner or saint, "separate and apart from the word." If "Spirit of God uses means over and beyond the revealed will of God in persuading men…then the word of God is not sufficient."[54] The "Spirit does not have to be here in person to teach, rule and guide by His word any more than Blackstone must be here to rule, guide or settle a point of law." [55] The work of the Spirit is thus reduced to mere cognition.

These statements horrified many. Burnett called it the "word alone doctrine" or "Spirit-in-the-word theory." "They have the idea," he wrote, "that the thought or idea in the word is the Holy Spirit."[56] In contrast to past Restoration luminaries (e.g., Campbell, Benjamin Franklin, Moses Lard, T. W. Brents), the position of the *FF*, according to Burnett, "admit[s] that the sectarians were right" about "the reformation" in that "we have no Holy Ghost." The *FF* "is so shy of the sectarian theory of the Spirit alone that [it] has switched off on the other side of the track to the word-alone doctrine." Burnett contends for a "Spirit-and-word theory" where the Spirit "dwells in the temple or church of God on earth today" and wields the word as a sword.[57]

Harding considered this such an important question that the denial of the personal indwelling Spirit, who enables transformed living, was tantamount to infidelity or at least "semi-infidel[ity]."[58] Such a denial is a "withering, deadly curse to those that believe it."[59] "Does the Holy Spirit do anything now except what the Word does?" Harding asks. "Do we get help, any kind or in any way,

---

[54] Denton, "The Spirit and the Word," *FF* 21 (4 July 1905) 1.

[55] Denton, "Question and Answer," *FF* 21 (29 August 1905) 1.

[56] T. R. Burnett, "Owen to the Rescue," *GA* 40 (21 April 1898) 251.

[57] Burnett, "On the Holy Spirit," *FF* 20 (10 May 1904) 3. This article is followed by an editor's note from George Savage: "The Holy Ghost operates on both saint and sinner. It does it by teaching. This teaching is in the Bible." Also "Burnett's Budget," *GA* 40 (14 July 1898) 443: "You have proved the charge made by the sectarians for fifty years, that you do not believe in the Holy Spirit at all. No Spirit in the body, except the ideas contained in the word."

[58] Harding, "Another Effort to Get Dr. Holloway Out of the Fog," *CLW* 19 (24 October 1905) 8.

[59] Harding, "Saving Souls, Special Providence, Dr. Holloway," *CLW* 21 (29 January 1904) 8.

from God except what we get by studying the Bible?"⁶⁰ Scripture alone, then, is not sufficient for Christian living.

> Scripture does not teach the Bible alone thoroughly furnishes the man of God for every good work, but that the Bible in addition to what had already been given does so...I am as far as the East is from the West from believing that neither God, Christ, nor the Holy Spirit can help us except by talking to us.⁶¹

In his discussion with Holloway, Harding asks, "has not Dr. Holloway yet learned that we need more than knowledge?"⁶² Christians need wisdom, power, and love for living in God's kingdom, and these come only through the Holy Spirit. "Mark you," wrote Harding, "it does not matter how much you may read the Bible, nor how much you delight in it."⁶³ This will not keep Christians from stumbling. The Spirit is the believer's divine enabler and transformer. The specific point was whether there was any power available to the Christian other than ideas, cognition or epistemic awareness. Harding, among others, thought so.

The "word-only" theory ultimately won the day and became the general consensus among churches of Christ in the 1940s-1950s, though it was not an absolute one (e.g., H. Leo Boles, Gus Nichols, and K. C. Moser). However, a "wild democracy" re-emerged in the 1960s as the papers once again debated the nature of the Spirit's indwelling and function.

Conclusion

A "wild democracy" characterized churches of Christ from 1880 into the 1930s. The discussions were vigorous, often filled with sarcasm, and sometimes bitter, but it was usually free and tolerant. Intolerance emerged when conformity and uniformity became the goal rather than unity. Ultimately, conformity, achieved in the

---

⁶⁰ Harding, "Questions and Answers," *The Way* 4 (17 July 1902) 123.

⁶¹ Harding, "How Does God Help His People?" *CLW* 20 (6 February 1906) 8-9.

⁶² Harding, "Fog," 8.

⁶³ Harding, "The Holy Spirit: Does He Dwell in Us? What Does He Do for Us?" *CLW* 19 (13 June 1905) 9.

1940s-1950s, suppressed this "wild democracy," which pushed non-institutional churches out the door just as premillennialists were ushered out in the 1930s and 1940s.

When conformity in most particular—patterns of ecclesial theology, liturgy, and practice—becomes a "test of fellowship," then the freedom of the "wild democracy" disappears. Power structures, however they may exist, apply various pressures to produce and enforce agreement. Diversity subverts the envisioned uniformity. Any divergence from the uniform consensus must, according to those in power, entail a loss of fellowship.

This was not how many of our theological ancestors thought. Alexander Campbell, though he believed there was such a thing as an "ancient order" for the church, did not think conformity to that "ancient order" was a "test of fellowship" or necessary for unity among fellow Christians. He is quite explicit about this. Campbell "never made" compliance to the ancient order "a test of christian [sic] character or terms of christian [sic] communion."[64]

F. D. Srygley, whom Lipscomb appointed the front page editor of the *GA* in 1881 though they disagreed about missionary societies, knew varied opinions would exist in any community seeking truth. Unity does not depend on conformity. On the contrary, it is rooted in the saving work of God. Consequently, "the basis of union ought always be as broad as the conditions of salvation. No man has any right to make his plea for union narrower than this. It is wrong to make anything a condition of fellowship which is not essential to salvation."[65]

J. N. Armstrong, Harding's son-in-law and the first president of Harding College, epitomized vibrant, free, and tolerant discussion. He championed the rights of people to speak freely without fear of exclusion.

> There is a great need to stress the importance of maintaining freedom of speech in the kingdom of God. Intolerance is dangerous to the future growth of the church...All progress of

---

[64] Campbell, "Replication No. II. to Spencer Clark," *Christian Baptist* 5 (3 September 1827) 370.

[65] F. D. Srygley, *The New Testament Church: Editorials of F. D. Srygley Which Appeared in the Gospel Advocate from 1889 to 1900*, compiled and edited by F. B. Srygley (Nashville: Gospel Advocate, 1955) 194.

truth…has always depended on free speech and progressive teachers who were not afraid to teach their honest convictions.[66]

Churches of Christ are uniquely suited for a "wild democracy." Such a democracy is good as long as it does not subvert authentic unity, which is rooted in God's saving work in Christ. Churches of Christ have the flexibility for a "wild democracy" because that democracy finds its unity in the deeper narrative of Scripture rather than in formalized creeds and institutionalized power structures. Our union is the confession of God's acts revealed in Scripture: God has acted in Christ through the Spirit for the salvation of the world.

I remain in churches of Christ because its polity, original vision, and diverse history permit a free, energetic, and devout search for truth. This search, however, must embrace the practice of love, which is an authentic mark of discipleship. The discussion must share a common narrative, the biblical story of God's redemptive work through Christ in the power of the Spirit. When believers love each other and share a common narrative rooted in Christ, a "wild democracy" empowers open discussion.

Of course, the content of that "common narrative," the narrative of God in Jesus, becomes a crux. It is the story of the gospel embodied in the life of Jesus, proclaimed by the apostles in Acts (e.g., Acts 10:34-43), and lived within early Christian communities (reflected in the epistles). God created heaven and earth, chose Israel to bless the nations, incarnated the Word through the appearance of Jesus of Nazareth, poured out the Spirit upon renewed Israel, and leads the people of God to the hope of new creation.

This life with a "common narrative" must, however, embrace tolerance. This is something we sorely lack today, whether religiously or politically. We hear shrill voices, condemnations, and anger more than we hear gentle and kind discussion. Tolerance does not mean we accept all and any beliefs since we confess a common narrative, but it does mean we love each other and seek common cause in God's kingdom. This is the kind of tolerance

---

[66] Quoted in L. C. Sears, *For Freedom: A Biography of John Nelson Armstrong* (Austin, TX: Sweet, 1969) 276.

I Stayed for the Wild Democracy

Armstrong envisioned in one of his most profound articles entitled "United, Yet Divided":[67]

> I suppose no one ever met a man who came up to the perfect life of Christ in his conduct. Neither did any one ever see, read or hear of a church so perfectly one as Christ and the Father. Before such a church could be, every member must be perfect in knowledge and must hold the truth without error; or all must hold the same truth and the same error; and they must develop alike every day or the union will be destroyed.
>
> These are impossibilities, for there are babes, boys and girls, men and women, in Christ, hence the different degrees of development and the varied imperfections that must necessarily exist in every church. Then it is expecting too much to expect perfection in union among such imperfections and developments. Individual growth must continue. Each individual conscience must be respected and left free. On the fundamental principles of Christ the church does agree, and has always agreed. Whenever a man takes Jesus as Lord we are to bear with him in his weakness and wait for him to grow, regardless of his errors and false doctrines. The church at Corinth had members who believed there were other gods than the true God."

A "wild democracy" is a good thing—though it may be a "wild ride"—as long as love abounds, freedom is encouraged, and the mighty acts of God are confessed.

---

[67] Armstrong, "United, Yet Divided," *The Way* 4 (14 August 1902) 156-157.

I Stayed for the Wedding

Chris Altrock[1]

My life is a journey between two weddings: one from which I derived and one toward which I'm drawn. Events connected to the first wedding mark one of the most significant milestones in my life. Circumstances related to the second wedding will evidence an even more significant waypost.

The Wedding From Which I Derived

I am literally the result of an event I didn't attend—the wedding of my mom and dad. I have no memories of the ceremony. For me, the day existed only in black and white photographs in an album in our wood-paneled living room atop the Sacramento Mountains in my childhood home of Sunspot, New Mexico. But that day eventually gave birth to my twin brother Craig and me. I owe my life to the union blessed at that service.

The dissolution of that same marriage also gave birth to a kind of death within me. I have vivid memories of the formal ending of the marriage between my mom and dad. Craig and I sat in the marble-lined courthouse in Alamogordo, New Mexico. The disharmony of my parent's marital discord playing out in the courtroom was muffled by the thickness of oak doors and the thumping of

---

[1] Chris Altrock is the author of seven books. He provides spiritual direction and trains others in spiritual direction. He has preached for the Highland Church of Christ in Memphis, TN since 1998. He and his wife Kendra have two children.

our own hearts as we waited outside the doors. Inside, a judge decided if we would continue to attend our fourth grade class with Mrs. Clark and live with our Basenji named Kolo and our dad, or if we would move miles away to Las Cruces to live with our mom and attend new schools, or if, for the first time in our lives, we would be separated and live in different homes.

The judge ruled in favor of keeping the womb-mates roommates and in favor of granting our father custody. We hopped in the station wagon to drive home with dad, and mom, eyes red from weeping, drove out of the parking lot, empty-handed and brokenhearted.

Little did I know how much my own heart was also breaking—because when you live with dad and your twin in a village nine thousand feet on top of a mountain, and your mom now lives in a desert next to the Rio Grande, she can't just drop by on a whim and take you to get ice cream. Visits require major planning. Suddenly the mom who made every meal, who was home when you jumped off the school bus, who gave hugs and kisses at night, wasn't there. You see her a few weekends during school and two months in the summer. But the empty chair every night at the dinner table, especially early on, reflects an even emptier place in your heart.

Especially when you have no God to fill it.

Augustine famously wrote, "Thou hast made us for thyself, O Lord, and our heart is restless until it finds its rest in thee."[2] This is bad news for a youngster with a restless heart and no God to tame it. That's what my mom's departure had done—unmoored my heart. It began to rock in the waves of grief with no heavenly hand to steady it.

My parents gave Craig and me many good things. We had, in most respects, an idyllic childhood. The Lincoln National Forest was our backyard. Black bears, deer, raccoons, and hummingbirds were our neighbors. Wild raspberries and other berries were our fast foods. We lived among a community of scientists and their families who had moved to the peak from all over the planet to study the sun. Winters brought feet of powdery white snow on

---

[2] *Saint Augustine Confessions*, Oxford World's Classics (Henry Chadwick, Translator; Oxford University Press, 1998), p. 3.

which to ski and sled. Fall brought leaves in brilliant and bold colors. Spring and summer meant playing outdoors for hours with friends, riding bikes and hiking in the woods. My parents gave us this mountaintop paradise and their own love.

But they gave us neither God nor church. We never prayed at meal times. There was no Bible read aloud or in private at home. Sundays were for reading the rare paper delivered to Sunspot and for relaxing. We never knew the warm hugs of nursery workers or Sunday School teachers welcoming us into their classes. We never experienced the sacred songs sung so often they became a soundtrack. Sunspot had no church buildings. The closest church was forty minutes away in Cloudcroft. Once, Hubert and Marie, the postmasters in Sunspot, packed up all the kids and took us to Vacation Bible School at the Church of Christ in Cloudcroft. That was my first exposure to God and to church. But it was temporary. I never returned.

Thus when a sinkhole caused by my parent's divorce began to erode my heart, I had no supernatural resource upon which to rely. Unhindered, it grew. I was unconscious of this. Only years later did I recognize the full extent of this anti-Genesis moment—this uncreating going on within me. For those of you who have endured far more—drug addiction, the loss of family members by cancer or drunk drivers, or the searing pain of poverty—my loss may seem minuscule. But grief has its own way with each of us. And the gravity of grief, if given any incline, can turn almost any snowball into a snowslide. It chose to within me. Physically, it tore a hole in my stomach—I developed a stomach ulcer. Emotionally, it ripped a hole in my heart.

In my teen years, I found myself obsessed with the three A's—approval, affection and attention. From coaches. From teachers. From girls. Each "A" was an attempt to fill what had become an empty quarry in my heart. But it was like tossing rocks into the Grand Canyon. And while externally, and in certain interior locations, my life was pleasant and happy, in the most central places inside of me it was, as in those days of Narnia, "always winter and never Christmas."[3]

---

[3] C. S. Lewis, *The Lion, The Witch and The Wardrobe* (HarperCollins, 2005), 60.

More accurately, the restlessness caused by the absence of Mom awakened me to a much deeper restlessness caused by the absence of my Maker. I know now that he *was* present. He is always present. But I was not present to him. This hunger for a mother's love sensitized me to a love for something else I couldn't name, but something that not even a mother's love could quench. No human approval, affection or attention would ever fill.

This was my plight, created, in part, from that first wedding, that "I do" between my parents.

The Wedding Toward Which I'm Drawn

And God used Churches of Christ to reveal that this ache would only be resolved by a wedding yet to be.

In *Fiddler on the Roof* Hodel sings,

> Matchmaker, Matchmaker,
> Make me a match,
> Find me a find,
> catch me a catch
> Matchmaker, Matchmaker
> Look through your book,
> And make me a perfect match.[4]

Hodel lived in a culture which believed in the need for an intermediary to introduce young adults to those to whom their hearts were best suited. In the same way, I stood desperately in need of a matchmaker who could lead me to the one to whom my heart was best suited. Though I could not articulate that unconscious desire at the time, and although I did not know that Jesus was the groom and I was a bride, the divine wedding which is the *telos* of the entire human narrative was the underlying ache I was feeling within. This wedding which shows up again and again in the last book of that Bible I'd not yet read yet was the cure to the disease from which was suffering:

---

[4] *Fiddler on the Roof: Vocal Selections* Jerry Bock (Composer), Sheldon Harnick (Composer) Hal Leonard (August 1, 1983).

- "Let us rejoice and exult and give him the glory, for the marriage of the Lamb has come, and his Bride has made herself ready…" (Revelation 19:7 ESV)
- "And I saw the holy city, new Jerusalem, coming down out of heaven from God, prepared as a bride adorned for her husband." (Revelation 21:2 ESV)
- "Then came one of the seven angels who had the seven bowls full of the seven last plagues and spoke to me, saying, 'Come, I will show you the Bride, the wife of the Lamb.'" (Revelation 21:9 ESV)
- "The Spirit and the Bride say, 'Come.' And let the one who hears say, 'Come.' And let the one who is thirsty come; let the one who desires take the water of life without price." (Revelation 22:17 ESV)

This was the love and the life for which I was meant. The ache I felt in my heart would only ultimately be cured by this love.

Churches of Christ became my matchmaker, introducing me to this groom, cultivating my heart for him, forming within me the ways for drawing ever closer to him, and becoming a sacramental community in which his presence became ever more real.

I realized for the first time in my life that the approval, affection, and applause I'd been missing and seeking at home and everywhere else was available in its purest and sweetest form from the groom Jesus. I saw that Christianity was not about rules and religion. It was about romance—the invitation to a wedding which would fill the broken heart within me.

This view of Christian spirituality as romance came into clarity over the course of several years through figures like John of the Cross and Julian of Norwich. John of the Cross was a Spanish priest who became a widely read author of several works. His *Spiritual Canticle* was composed when he was imprisoned and tortured in a tiny cell (1577). In it he wrote poetically of himself in search of the great love of his life, Jesus:[5]

11. Reveal your presence,
and may the vision of your beauty be my death;

---

[5] John of the Cross, *A Spiritual Canticle of the Soul and the Bridegroom Christ* (CreateSpace Independent Publishing, 2013).

for the sickness of love
is not cured
except by your very presence and image.

26. In the inner wine cellar
I drank of my Beloved, and, when I went abroad
through all this valley
I no longer knew anything,
and lost the herd that I was following.

27. There he gave me his breast;
 there he taught me a sweet and living knowledge;
and I gave myself to him,
keeping nothing back;
there I promised to be his bride.

28. Now I occupy my soul
and all my energy in his service;
I no longer tend the herd,
nor have I any other work
now that my every act is love.

John was so enamored with Jesus that it was like a sickness–and only Jesus was the cure. Jesus was like a fine wine that John drank and drank–he consumed Jesus. John was so drawn to Jesus that he withheld nothing from Jesus. He gave his entire self to Jesus. And now every act done in the body was an act of love for Jesus.

Julian of Norwich was an English ascetic who devoted herself to prayer and spiritual counsel. Her first book *Revelations of Divine Love* (ca. 1395) was one of the first books written by a woman in the English language. Notice Julian's focus on love:[6]

> When I was thirty years old and a half, God sent me a bodily sickness in which I lay three days and three nights…and on the third night I expected often to have passed away…and being still in youth, I thought it a great sadness to die— not for anything that was on earth that pleased me to live for, nor

---

[6] Julian of Norwich, *Revelations of Divine Love*, Oxford World's Classics (Barry Windeatt, Transl; Oxford University Press, 2015).

for any pain that I was afraid of (for I trusted in God of His mercy) but because I would have liked to have lived so that I could have loved God better and for a longer time. (Reading Three, Chapter Three)

I saw that He is to us everything that is good and comfortable for us. He is our clothing which for love enwraps us, holds us, and all encloses us because of His tender love, so that He may never leave us. And so in this showing I saw that He is to us everything that is good, as I understood it. (Reading Eight, Chapter Five)

God wishes to be known, and He delights that we remain in Him, because all that is less than He is not enough for us. And this is the reason why no soul is at rest until it is emptied of everything that is created. When the soul is willingly emptied for love in order to have Him who is all, then is it able to receive spiritual rest. (Reading Nine)

…for truly our Lover desires that our soul cleave to Him with all its might and that we evermore cleave to His goodness, for of all things that heart can think, this pleases God most and soonest succeeds. (Reading Twelve)

and therefore we can ask of our Lover with reverence all that we wish, for our natural wish is to have God and the good wish of God is to have us. (Reading Thirteen)

The entire reason for living, and living longer, for Julian, is to love God better and longer. God's love enwraps us like clothing. His love alone is sufficient for us and greater than all else to which we might cling. It is our greatest wish.

This love, this wedding, was the ultimate goal for which we were made. This was the longing, the aching I had noticed in my heart. This was the goal which the Bible pointed toward in its closing chapters.

Churches of Christ made this goal possible. Whether it was through the small rural Cloudcroft Church of Christ where I first learned of Jesus and was baptized, the college church of the University Church of Christ in Las Cruces, New Mexico, where I was deeply discipled and discerned a call to ministry, or the urban Highland Church of Christ in Memphis, Tennessee, where I learned service to the poor, spiritual formation, and the transformation that comes through suffering, Churches of Christ led me into the spiritual romance for which all humans are made.

The Matchmaker of Sacraments

In particular, Churches of Christ have been a matchmaker for me through three ways: sacraments, saints, and surrogates. Each of these three has enabled me to more deeply know Jesus and draw near to my eventual wedding with him.

First, through the sacramental ordinances of baptism, the Lord's Supper, and the assembly we experience the gracious presence and activity of God, I encountered Jesus in ever-deepening ways—as Lipscomb professor John Mark Hicks has helped us understand.[7]

Although at times Churches of Christ have approached the assembly, communion, and baptism based on our human role in them (what we do), the real treasure comes in the divine role in them (what God does). These three, Hicks has helped us recover, are, at their best in the Restoration Movement, "sacraments." They are sacraments in that the concrete realities of water (baptism), bread and juice (communion) and gathered people (the worship assembly), point beyond themselves to something else and become a means of grace in which God, Christ, and the Spirit encounter us in transformative ways.

Churches of Christ, at their worst, have made these three barriers to divine romance. French author Bernard of Clairvaux, in his treatise *On the Love of God* writes of the Christian journey as a maturing through four "degrees" of love.[8] The Christian faith is about love, primarily loving God. We could call it a romance. But this romance begins, in Barnard's words, with the "love of self for self's sake." Many in the human race never live beyond this self-centered love. Even those who come to faith in Christ, though they may

---

[7] John Mark Hicks, *Come to the Table* (Leafwood, 2008); John Mark Hicks and Greg Taylor, *Down to the River to Pray* (Leafwood, 2004); John Mark Hicks, Johnny Melton & Bobby Valentine, *A Gathered People* (Leafwood, 2007).

[8] Saint Bernard of Clairvaux, *On the Love of God* (Aeterna Press, 2015).

appear to mature past love of self for self's sake, simply manage to replace it with its cousin—the "love of God for self's sake." We love God. Yet we love him primarily because he becomes the means to gain what we selfishly desire. He becomes the means to our ends. Sadly, this often shows up most clearly in the sacraments of worship.

The word "war" has been attached to "worship" perhaps more often than anything else in our congregations in the past three decades as we've wrestled between those who want to argue that New Testament worship is restored when it looks and sounds like something from the 1950's and 1960's and those who press that worship practices must be allowed to incarnate themselves in forms and expressions appropriate to the current time. Highland has been written up by various watchdogs and gatekeepers for the appearance of praise teams, videos, handclapping, and women in corporate worship. Even after more than twenty years of full-time ministry, I still often receive letters or emails of complaint. The vast majority are concerned with the assembly and are from a member of our tribe—usually from someone visiting from another Church of Christ. I still laugh at the recent note from a visiting couple who took time to complain that the communion bread in our late service, lovingly home-made and freshly-baked by members of that service, was too dissimilar from the matzos in their church. When our late service is over, most of our attendees run to grab what's left over. It's that good! But this couple could only complain because it wasn't store-bought factory-made matzos. Rather than worship being a place of sacramental encounter with God, it becomes a place where we seek to use God to get what we want—a church that does worship exactly as we want it done, where everything is predictable, done according to our personal preferences, and aligned with our opinions regarding what is appropriate.

Yet, at our best, in my personal experience, these three sacraments have been transformative matchmakers. Time and time again I've found baptism, weekly communion, and the worship assembly in Churches of Christ to be the ways in which I've been led deeper and deeper into a romance with Christ. Each summer when I watch dozens of teens baptized at Camp Highland, each week when I listen to a Highland couple or individual testify before communion, and every Sunday whether it's worship in the traditional, contemporary or modern services at Highland, I am repeatedly drawn more deeply in love with this lamb, this lion, this King, this Messiah who lived, died and rose for us.

When I rest silently and replay the years of my divine romance, I can still hear the words of specific sermons preached by specific preachers from our movement that fueled the fire of my love for Christ—Max Lucado, Marlon McWilliams, Grant Standefer, Harold Shank, Randy Harris, Don McLaughlin, Buddy Bell, Mike Cope, Landon Saunders, Harold Hazelip, Mark Hamilton, Jack Reese, Rick Achtley, Jerry Taylor and others. I can still feel the emotions surrounding the worship experiences led by specific worship leaders—Brishan Hatcher, David Ralston, Zach Thomas, and others. I can still taste the bread and juice at very specific communion moments. And I can still recall the tears, smiles, hugs, shouts, splashes, and praises of very specific people or persons being baptized. These sacraments, a weekly occurrence in Churches of Christ, have been a matchmaker. They are ushering me into the wedding toward which I am growing.

The Matchmaker of Saints

Second, through saints in Churches of Christ, I've grown in my experience of Jesus' love for me and my expression of my own love for Jesus. While the word "sacrament" above and the word "saint" here are not often used in our tribe, I'm using saint here as it's used in the New Testament. The church is comprised solely and simply of saints (Rom. 1:7; 1 Cor. 1:2; 2 Cor. 1:1; Eph. 1:1; Phil. 1:1; Col. 1:2).

No doubt, there are times when members of our churches act less than saintly. In 2012, citizens of the Mid South opened their Sunday paper and their Tuesday paper to find a full-page ad which ran this headline "The Whole Truth About Homosexuality."[9] The advertisement said it was paid for by "Memphis Churches of Christ and Interested Individuals." The ad was a selected series of Scriptures with commentary which spoke of divine judgment and wrath upon homosexuals. It created a firestorm of controversy in the

---

[9] http://www.wmcactionnews5.com/story/19981860/mid-south-newspaper-ad

Memphis area. The gay community responded in a particularly intriguing way. Rather than lashing out at Churches of Christ, they held a food drive, hoping to contrast their posture with the one shown in the ad.

Two things were particularly distressing. First, the ad itself was deeply theologically short-sighted. If Christians had one shot at a one-page ad directed to the non-Christian world regarding God's view of homosexuals, what was written on that page was definitely not an effective nor a Gospel-centered message. Second, no one had bothered to contact us before publishing the ad, yet it claimed to be from Memphis Churches of Christ. When we did our own detective work, we discovered that, in fact, it had come from a small handful of Christians in one Church of Christ in the area. Ultimately, we learned, it came from a single church leader.

Thankfully, we had connections with the local NBC affiliate, and we were able to write a response which was briefly included in the evening news and was included in full on their website. It read as follows:

> On behalf of Memphis-area Churches of Christ, I'd like to say the following: disregard anyone claiming to speak for Churches of Christ. Several days ago a full-page ad appeared in the Commercial Appeal. Its author indicated that the ad was presented on behalf of area Churches of Christ. The flyer claimed to present the view of these congregations regarding same-sex attraction. Ironically, Churches of Christ are non-denominational. That's a religious way of saying we have no formal superstructure, no official bishops, representatives or the like. For one person or group to claim to speak for Churches of Christ is a bit like me claiming to speak for Memphis when I vote next Tuesday. My vote speaks only for me. Each congregation in Churches of Christ speaks only for itself. Anyone familiar with the history of non-denominational groups like Churches of Christ would know it would be a miracle to meet with the nearly ninety congregations in metro-Memphis and bring them to agreement on a written document like the Commercial Appeal ad. We've fussed over things much less significant (of course, we're not the only group to do so). No such meeting took place. No such miracle was recorded. Churches of Christ, and other Christian congregations

in the U. S., have the perception of being repressive, exclusive and intolerant. Young people are leaving institutional Christianity by droves. There's not an ad, no matter the author, that can adequately address these concerns. And, by the way, if I were going to take a page out in the Commercial Appeal, I'd probably speak of the transforming love of Jesus for all. So, if you'd like to know what people in Churches of Christ think about an issue like homosexuality, don't look for an answer in the paper. Visit a minister or elder at a local congregation. Go to lunch. Have coffee. Talk one on one with a real person. Who knows, you may just be pleasantly surprised at what you find."

We've got some less-than-saintly people in our pews. But we do have some saints. And a lot of them. And time and time again they've been the matchmakers God has used to draw me more deeply into Christ. When I close my eyes and replay the years of my romance with Christ, a virtual parade of saints marches before me—men and women who have fleshed out for me what it looks like to be passionately in love with Jesus and in love with humanity:

E.H. Ijams, long-time Highland minister who nurtured a love for Scripture and for God in his ministry at Highland;

Larry McKenzie, another long-time minister at Highland who remains on staff after close to fifty years and who models deep love and passionate prayer;

Joe Cannon, a legendary missionary based at Highland whose devotion to Christ and faith-filled praying still rings in my years;

Carl McKelvey, longtime Lipscomb University professor and leader whose enthusiasm for the spiritual life inspires me and thousands of others;

Gary Holloway, executive director of World Convention of Churches of Christ and author whose example, teaching and books on prayer and the spiritual life and whose spiritual direction have deeply impacted me;

Wilma and Wesley Lane, whose authentic love for Christ in my early days of faith in Cloudcroft, New Mexico, were some of my first glimpses into what the spiritual life could be;

Byron Fike, my campus minister at New Mexico State University, who taught me what a "quiet time" was and why it was the most important time of the day;

Stanna Porter, whose devotion to Christ in prayer, study, service, and compassion at the University Church of Christ in Las Cruces, New Mexico, greatly inspired me;

Jack Spray, the elder at the University Church of Christ, who taught me by his remarkable life, the kind of impact an elder in a church could have by kneeling in prayer and washing feet rather than calling the shots or withholding permission;

David Harrelson, youth minister at the University Church of Christ in Las Cruces, New Mexico, whose tireless love for every generation during decades of service in that congregation revealed to me an entirely new standard of love;

Ann King, the quiet woman of prayer at Highland to whom people came from around the country for spiritual guidance and counsel;

Beverly Ralston, a woman who has taught and modeled prayer at Highland for decades;

Lawana Maxwell, Highland women's minister, whose passionate and persistent quest to call women and men at Highland deeper into God has challenged me personally and whose partnership has enabled me to do the same;

Ron Wade, Highland elder, whose devotion to prayer, fasting, silence, and compassion, even in the midst of the busiest schedule I have ever seen, continues to amaze me;

Earl Lavender, Lipscomb professor and founding director of the Institute for Christian Spirituality, whose spiritual mentoring drew me into deep places.

Randy Harris, professor at Abilene Christian University, whose long-term spiritual mentoring pushed me and pulled me into spiritual disciplines I'd never even heard about and helped me experience Christ profoundly;

Jackie Halstead, director of Selah, whose spiritual direction helped me to encounter Christ in silence and solitude in ways that were transformative.

Rhonda Lowry, Lipscomb professor, whose teaching on prayer and spiritual formation has been a consistent nudge deeper and deeper into Christ.

This is just my personal list, and only a partial one at that. As a movement, we have a similar list. Churches of Christ have numerous saints who, over the centuries, have pointed all our congregations by example and by teaching, to the wedding to which we are all growing. Each one is a remarkable matchmaker.

The Matchmaker of Surrogates

A surrogate is someone who stands in for another. A third way in which Churches of Christ have served as a particularly powerful matchmaker for me is by their offering of surrogates. I've been blessed to be part of congregations who were willing to point me to spiritual surrogates—people who stood outside our movement and who could provide something which our movement could not.

I acknowledge that my experience does not match everyone's within Churches of Christ. I've visited numerous congregations where the church libraries were excised of any books that were not authored by members of our tribe. I recall speaking once at a gathering of Church of Christ members where participant after participant criticized the Catholic faith—and then I quoted from a handful of Catholic spiritual leaders in my presentation! One participant walked out, in part, because of this. Not all within our movement have been comfortable acknowledging the rich spiritual resources available in the Christian streams outside ours. Thankfully, my experience has been different.

Leaders in the campus ministry at the University Church of Christ in Las Cruces, NM gave me a copy of J. I. Packer's *Knowing God* for my birthday when I was a college student. It was, I believe, the first non-Church of Christ spiritual book I'd ever read. And it was transformative. Those leaders realized Packer would grant me something no one else within our movement could.

That was the first of what would become a friendly flood of surrogates. During the next decades, saints in Churches of Christ would introduce me to Dallas Willard, John Ortberg, John of the Cross, Julian of Norwich, Richard Foster, Ruth Haley Barton, Martin Laird, Thomas Merton, Richard Rohr, Henri Nouwen, Philip Yancey, Timothy Keller, N. T. Wright, Scot McKnight, St Benedict, Phyllis Tickle, Barbara Taylor Brown, St Ignatius, Jan Johnson, and many others. Each stood outside our tradition and brought a perspective very different from ours. Each led me deeper into the heart of Christ. I was deeply blessed to be part of churches that did not dismiss these simply because they were not part of Churches of Christ but rather viewed them as partners and fellow travelers. Each stood in for our own saints, granting me views of Christ before unseen, giving me understanding not necessarily available in our own tradition.

God has many matchmakers. In my journey, He used Churches of Christ. God used a high school senior named Gary Cox who was a member of the Cloudcroft Church of Christ to lead me to the point of baptism when I was a high school sophomore striving unsuccessfully to fill a void contributed to by the absence of my mom but rooted in the absence of a relationship with my Maker. And ever since, God's used Churches of Christ through sacraments, saints and surrogates to lead me nearer and nearer to that final and ultimately soul-fulfilling wedding with Christ. Why would I even think of leaving?

I Stayed for the Light

Ron Highfield[1]

My journey with Churches of Christ began the day I was born, and I do not expect it to end until the day I am laid to rest. My grandfather on my mother's side was a poor Nazarene preacher who earned most of his living as a Mississippi farmer. Grandpa Shippey was born with only one good arm; doctors amputated the useless limb when he was a child. After my mother reached 15 or 16 years of age, she drove her father to his preaching appointments until she left for Trevecca Nazarene College in Nashville, Tennessee. When my father returned from serving in WWII, he became a farmer in Northeast Alabama. His family had roots in the Restoration Movement on the Christian Church side, but he was not attending church when he met my mother. They met when my Grandpa moved to Alabama to preach for a small, rural Methodist Church. At that time, my father smoked and chewed tobacco, and my mother informed him that she would have nothing to do with

---

[1] Ron Highfield is Professor of Religion at Pepperdine University where he has taught for the past 28 years. He received the B.A. in Bible from Harding University, the M.Th. from Harding School of Theology, and the M.A. and Ph.D. in Religious Studies from Rice University. Ron served as a minister in churches of Christ in West Virginia, Arkansas, and Texas before moving to California. He has authored academic articles in such journals as the *Restoration Quarterly*, *Stone-Campbell Journal*, *Christian Scholar's Review*, *Theological Studies*, and *The Journal for the Evangelical Theological Society*. He is the author of *Great is the Lord: Theology for the Praise of God* (Eerdmans, 2008), *God, Freedom & Human Dignity: Embracing A God-Centered Identity in a Me-Centered Culture* (InterVarsity Press, 2013), and *The Faithful Creator: Affirming Creation and Providence in an Age of Anxiety* (InterVarsity Press 2015). He and his wife Martha Farrar Highfield have two sons.

someone with such filthy habits. He quit smoking, and they were married in April 1950. I arrived in June of 1951.

Until that time my father had attended with my mother at the Methodist church where her father preached. But my birth caused him to reassess his life. He convinced my mother to attend the Fort Payne Church of Christ. Thus it began that my life was surrounded and enfolded in the arms of the Church of Christ. My life was punctuated with church meetings, Sunday school, vacation Bible schools and Gospel meetings. Sunday mornings, Sunday evenings and Wednesday evenings our family packed into our 1949 Plymouth and drove nine miles to church. At home, there was no cursing, smoking, or drinking. There was Bible reading, hymn singing, and religious discussion. My mother was faithful, unselfish, and thrifty. But I was a boy, and so my father was and is—even 46 years after his untimely death—the greatest human influence in my life. He was a good man and was known by all as a good man. I had no doubt that he based his entire life on his Christian faith. I could see the beauty and moral strength of his character, and I wanted to be like him.

Call Into Ministry

As a young child, I loved learning the facts of the Bible. Being fairly intelligent, I picked it up pretty easily. I remember a girl at church about my age speaking of me as "the boy with the Bible background." When I was six years old, I told my first-grade teacher I wanted to be a preacher when I grew up. I don't know when it happened, but I changed my mind by my 10th birthday. I decided, rather, that I wanted to be a math teacher and a farmer. I think I came to view preachers as unmanly. My father's hands were calloused and strong. Preachers just didn't fit my image of a real man. There was in the rural South an old joke about there being three sexes: male, female, and preacher. And this country boy wanted to be all male!

Then at 13 years old, I had a disturbing experience. At the annual Vacation Bible School, the teenage boys were taught by a well-known and—to my mind—ancient preacher. Apparently, I displayed a wide-ranging familiarity with the Scriptures, so much so that that old preacher got an idea into his head. On the last night of the VBS, as we exited the church building after the closing assembly, this old man laid his hand on my shoulder, looked me straight in the eyes and said in a heavy Southern Appalachian accent I won't try to imitate in print, "Son, I think you ought to be a preacher." I was dumbfounded and could feel the blood rush to my face. I went home that evening hoping against hope that this old man had *not* spoken with the voice of God. I don't remember how long it took, but I eventually shook off this fear and continued with my life. I won't go into the events that took place between 13 and 18 years of age except to say that my father died suddenly shortly after my 17th birthday. In death as in life, my father had a profound impact on me. His death rekindled and solidified my desire to be like him.

My 2½ year experience at Freed-Hardeman College proved very positive for me. Though I was a math major, most of my friends were Bible majors, and we loved to engage in theological discussions and debates. After transferring to Harding College, I changed my major from math to chemistry but kept drawing my closest friends from within the Bible Department. My deal with God was this: I will make my living teaching chemistry or math in college and preach some on the weekends. But my personal interest in biblical studies and theology grew, and my desire to study chemistry waned. At the end of the fall semester of 1972, I was looking forward very much to the holidays, not to rest but to read religious books. During the 3-week Christmas break, I read 13 books and the entire New Testament. When I returned to school, I was even less excited about studying and teaching science.

About this time, the Harding Bible majors' Timothy Club met for the first time of the semester. The speaker was a very well-known preacher, and I went to hear him. I don't recall his topic. But I remember that at some point in his talk he said something like this: "and if you think you can fulfill your responsibility to God by preaching part-time, you are dead wrong...." At that moment, it was as if he were speaking directly to me. I was completely stunned and knew instantly that my deal with God had been rejected. I stepped out into the cold winter night without speaking to anyone. I walked to the Harding football field, climbed to the top of the bleachers and wrestled with God. Finally, I stood up and looked into the sky and yelled—at least it felt like yelling—"I give up!" God had closed every door but one and stood at my back pressing me onward. I had no choice. C. S. Lewis said of the day of his conversion that he was the most reluctant convert in England. And that night I was a very reluctant recruit to the ministry. But the next morning I dutifully changed my major to Bible.

After my undergraduate years, I spent a year as an associate minister in West Virginia. During that year, I visited with a campus minister at the West Virginia University at Morgantown who possessed a Master of Theology degree from Harding Graduate School of Religion. To be honest, I felt inferior and envious. So, I decided to move to Memphis and continue my education. On the way, however, I began to question my motives for wanting to attend graduate school. "Why am I doing this?" I asked myself. Am I doing it to prepare myself for service or to deal with my feelings of inferiority? Struggling with this question, I turned around and drove back home. After a few miserable days, it dawned on me: True, I cannot be sure that I have pure motives for wanting to attend graduate school, but I am no more certain of my motives for not attending graduate school! So, I got into my car and returned to Memphis. Again, it was not my wisdom and goodness that guided me to make the best decision. God simply blocked off all other routes.

My Experiences of Churches of Christ

Childhood

As a small child, my experience of church consisted of Sunday school and Wednesday evening Bible classes, the Sunday assembly, and the yearly Vacation Bible School. I thrilled at the adventures of the heroes of the Old Testament, David, Elijah, and Daniel. I loved the images of Jesus holding the children and healing the sick. And I loved the song, "Jesus loves me, this I know, for the Bible tells me so." I knew Jesus loved me, and I loved him in return. We memorized the books of the Bible as soon as we could pronounce them, and a little later I learned the stories of creation, the patriarchs, the prophets, and the kings. We studied the story of the church told in Acts of the Apostles. Before I graduated from High

School, I could tell you the basic content of every book in the Bible, and for some of the books, I knew the theme of each chapter. As I look back on those years, there is no doubt that, other than my parents, the women who taught my church classes were the most powerful influences for good in my life.

The Teen Years

Until I was about 11 years old, I had no real sense of belonging to a church with a distinctive theological message and distinct practices. I don't remember being critical or accepting of other groups. My world was my parents and my congregation. I am sure I sat through many sermons on Sunday and in Gospel meetings critical of the doctrines of the surrounding denominations. But since I didn't listen to sermons, I didn't get the message. Even before I understood the theological message, however, I picked up what I would call "brand loyalty." As we would drive through Northwest Alabama, I remember feeling a sense of pride as we passed the many church buildings with the "Church of Christ Meets Here" signs out front. But after my eleventh or twelfth year I began to get clear on the theological message. The Church of Christ followed the biblical teaching about the plan of salvation, church governance, and worship whereas the denominations did not. We did not follow creeds, and we had the right name. And as I understood it at that time, converting our neighbors from their denominations to the Church of Christ was our main evangelistic task. I'd never met an atheist or a Jew.

College and Graduate School

My mother was a school teacher and my father, though having only a tenth-grade education, was a well-read man. Both encouraged me from childhood to attend college, and I never doubted that this was my destiny. I wanted a job like my mother's, and this required an education. My parents also encouraged me to attend a Christian college. I did not need any persuading on that account because I longed to be with other Christian young people. High School had been a trial. Although most of the kids attended some church, many were completely immersed in the culture of alcohol, sex, theft, vandalism, and filthy language.

Freed-Hardeman College was around 180 miles from our house. It seemed like a long way away. At FHC I found a community of young people who were serious about Christianity and the church. The teachers were good and kind people. I especially loved my tennis coach and math teacher Robert Witt and my chemistry professor Eugene Hibbett. Freed-Hardeman College mirrored my experience in church, that is, daily life interacting with students and teachers corresponded to my relationship with my Sunday school teachers. But there was also the militant defense of the teachings that distinguished us from the denominations. This face of the college was especially prominent during the week of the Bible Lectureship. During this week, hundreds of preachers and elders converged on Henderson, Tennessee, to hear well-known preachers, evangelists, and editors discuss the controversies of the day. It was an exciting time for those of us with ambitions for leadership in the church. Though at that time a "true believer," I felt even then that some of the rhetoric was too harsh and self-certain. All in all, I am grateful for my time at FHC (now FHU), and I pray God's blessings on the good work that goes on there.

After 2½ years at FHC, I transferred to Harding College in Searcy, Arkansas. I found at Harding a warm and welcoming environment. And I remember those two years as some of the best times of my life. Limits of time and space forbid me to tell you a tenth of the lessons I learned there. God became to me a real presence and conversation partner. And I think I began to understand at a deeper level the love and grace of God. For those of you who don't know anything about Harding's history, you should know that Harding's namesake James A. Harding and its first president, J. N. Armstrong came from a tradition of deep spirituality and strong faith in divine providence. That spirituality was still alive when I arrived in 1971, exemplified by such men as Leslie Burke and Andy T. Richie, Jr. Harsh rhetoric was almost totally absent from Harding College. Harding's teachers and administration were no doubt committed to the distinctive teachings of Churches of Christ, but it was not as central to its evangelistic message. Harding focused on preaching the gospel to the whole world. The Harding experience was transformative. Listening to Jim Woodroof, the preacher at the College Church of Christ, every Sunday for two years convinced me for the first time that the preaching event could transform lives. I had never been happier in my life. May God bless all of you who made it so!

I left Harding College in December 1973 for a position as an associate minister in a congregation in West Virginia. I will skip this story and say only that I learned many lessons the hard way. After a year, I began a master's degree at Harding Graduate School of Religion in Memphis, Tennessee. At HGSR, I found myself in the company of some of the best and brightest men and women I had ever known. It was a serious place. Jack P. Lewis, Annie Mae Alston, Earl West, Phillip Slate, Thomas B. Warren, W.B. West, Harold Hazelip, Carroll Osburn and others were very intent on socializing us into the world of scholarship. Though the faculty and staff were deeply committed Christians and conservative in their theology, I found myself having to take seriously critics of what I believed about the Bible, God, and Jesus Christ. I was not allowed to dismiss arguments and evidence simply because the conclusion did not fit with what I had been taught. I needed this discipline, and after a short period of resentment, I became grateful for it. But it made me realize that I needed to rethink from the ground up everything I had been taught. Things I thought were clear had become obscure, things I thought matters of knowledge had become matters of opinion, and things that had been certain for me, now seemed, if not doubtful, at least doubtable. But how, when and where can I carry out this project of rebuilding? I needed time, resources, and trustworthy conversation partners, for there is no shortcut to clarity, certainty, and peace.

The Ministry Years

But time waits for no one. I got married to Martha Ellen Farrar, and after 38 years we are still together. What an amazing partner! And I took a job as campus minister at the College Church of Christ in Searcy, Arkansas. That was in 1979. My wife held a position in the Harding College Department of Nursing. I was happy to be returning to my beloved Harding. But within two years, the College Church elders and I discovered that we were not compatible. Perhaps it was a different personal style, but there were also doctrinal disagreements—or misunderstandings. Perhaps it was because I was still working through the challenges forced on me by my graduate education. But I shall say no more about that. From my perspective, God works all things for the good of those who love him (Romans 8:28), and I bless the hand that guided me through those troubled waters.

In 1981, I became the youth minister at the Bering Drive Church of Christ in Houston, Texas. At that time Bering Drive was considered by some a "fringe" church. It was home to editors, board members, and contributors to *Mission Journal*, a progressive publication critical of traditional Churches of Christ. This congregation also encouraged equal participation of men and women in one of its two worship services. We found ourselves at home at Bering Drive. My education was valued, and I was given room to continue my quest to rethink my faith from the ground up. But I discovered that youth ministry was not my strength. I loved my students, and I think I did the best I knew how for them. But one of my friends concluded in retrospect, "Ron failed at youth ministry." I can't dispute her blunt assessment. I loved the preaching of my dear friend Bill Love. Lynn Mitchell, Jr. became my friend and mentor. Elders Dwain Evans, Fielding Fromberg, Buddy Garner and Rolf Johnson were reliable friends and advisors. "Bering," as all insiders call it, was the right place at the right time, a haven in the storm. To anticipate a later section, the Bering experience gave us hope that there would continue to be a place for us within Churches of Christ and I would have time to think through my faith. Thank you, my Bering friends!

Earlier, I told the story of my hesitation about becoming a "preacher," the unwelcome call and my reluctance to accept it. I have never doubted that call, but it has not turned out the way I envisioned at that time. In my first ministry position, I learned the vast difference between volunteer ministry and a paid ministry position. I was shocked to realize that my opinions, my dressing habits, and my exercise routine had become matters of church-wide concern. What I had done previously for the joy of it now became a means of livelihood and subject to evaluation by others. I discovered that a different, and sometimes strange, set of standards are applied to ministers as if ministers are supposed to become composite personalities created by piecing together the eccentricities of the members. Suddenly, my faith had become public property, and my duty to God had been fused with my self-incurred answerability to the church. I could not spend more time with close friends than I did with others lest I be accused of favoritism. If you had doubts, sins, and struggles, to whom could you confess them? And if your supposedly private conversations make their way back to your elders, you may be held as responsible for them as if you had proclaimed them from the rooftops. I discovered that I could not continue to live this way. I know every minister reading this understands exactly what I am saying. And every elder ought to take note and take care.

My Life as an Elder

We moved to Southern California in 1989 to begin teaching in the Religion Division at Pepperdine University. I began attending the University Church of Christ, which meets on the University campus. Dan Anders was the preacher at that time, and he is the main reason we chose to attend this congregation. After six years of attending the congregation and being granted tenure at the University, I was asked to join the eldership. That was 21 years ago. Just as being a paid minister differs dramatically from being a volunteer church worker, life as an elder differs markedly from life as a paid minister. Two or three differences stand out. Elders are usually focused for the long haul on their congregations. Ministers tend to keep their options open for new opportunities. Elders are not usually paid and don't need to worry about getting fired. Elders have to shepherd the ministers. Elders and ministers measure success differently. Ministers don't usually boast about how many divorces, church splits, and grave sins do not happen. Elders may feel success at simply holding a diverse body of people together in peace for 20 or 30 years. And elders, unlike other members and, to a great extent, unlike ministers, have to make difficult decisions for the whole church. I will say more about this later, but the responsibility of being an elder has made me more conservative and cautious.

The Joy of the Professorate

I've cherished the goal of becoming a professor since I was 18 years of age. And in 1984, at age 33, I began a Ph.D. program in religious studies at Rice University, Houston, Texas. I completed the degree in 1988 and in 1989 accepted Pepperdine University's offer of a position teaching religion. I am now in my 27th year of teaching, and I have no plans of retiring any time soon. I find teaching and writing more rewarding than anything I have ever done. I connect my teaching to that call into the ministry I received at Harding College. I think I can say without undue self-promotion that I am much better at teaching than I was at preaching or college and youth ministry, and I am much happier. I've taught over 5,000 students in my career. Many of my students are missionaries, preachers in Churches of Christ, and college professors in Christian Colleges. I like to think that I have made a difference in the lives of many students by helping to become more secure and thoughtful in their faith. In any case, that has been my goal.

Why I Remain in Churches of Christ

Why do I stay in Churches of Christ? The human heart is deep and its motives are complex. We cannot fathom the ways of God's providence. But I will try to explain to the best of my ability why I stay.

Personal Reasons

The Church of Christ is my home. As you read above, my mother and father took me as a baby to the Church of Christ. There I learned about Jesus and the Bible from my Sunday school teachers. I found my wife of 38 years. I made my closest friends in Christian colleges or in congregations where I attended. The lives of long-time members of Churches of Christ are woven together with many threads into a coat of many colors. We have the same heroes and villains. We speak the same language and sing the same songs. We know about the "five steps to salvation" and the five "acts of worship." We know the Book of Acts. We know how to sing a capella; indeed we know what the word "a capella" means! I understand its strengths and weaknesses. I know its history, its ideals, controversies, and its failings. It defines who I am. Even if I "left," I could never really leave. You cannot change the past. And I could never be any more than a visitor anywhere else.

Theological Reasons

The a capella Church of Christ is a tradition sustained and animated by devotion to an idea. More precisely, it is a tradition sustained and animated by an interlocking set of ideas. Some of those ideas belong to the common confession of nearly all Christian traditions, Orthodox, Catholic, and Protestant. I call it the "Great Tradition." We hold in common with the great tradition belief that God sent his Son into the world for our salvation, that Jesus died for our sins and rose from the dead for our justification. Jesus Christ is the Son of God, Lord, and Savior. We accept God's gracious invitation to be reconciled to him by faith, repentance, confession, and baptism. We sustain our faith by gathering with the church to remember and participate in Jesus' body and blood in the Lord's Supper and by listening to the Scriptures read and expounded. And we acknowledge that we are obligated to live holy and godly lives in hope of the glorious manifestation of the Lord and of eternal life with God. The Church of Christ of the past and today affirms these central and commonly held teachings. I don't have to become Roman Catholic or Orthodox or Presbyterian or Lutheran or Baptist to participate in authentic Christianity. I heard it in the Fort Payne Church of Christ as a child and I hear it in the University Church of Christ where I am now an elder.

Some ideas that sustain and animate Churches of Christ we share only with the Protestant tradition in distinction from the Roman Catholic tradition. Indeed we share much in common with the Reformed wing of Protestantism, and even more specifically, the Puritan wing of the Reformed tradition. We share the Protestant critique of the Roman Catholic view of tradition, its view of human merit and justification, its view of Mary and the Saints, its view of purgatory, and, of course, its view of the Papacy. With Protestants, we affirm the primacy of Scripture as the final authority for faith and practice, and we hold to justification by grace through faith. With the Reformed and Puritans, we give special attention to church order, specifically arguing for congregationalism and simplicity in worship. With Baptists, we argue against infant baptism and for believers' baptism. In sum, the Church of Christ consists of much more than its unique characteristics. It embodies the "catholic" faith and the Protestant reforms in a concrete and local form. As a member of the Church of Christ, I am united with the "one, holy, catholic, and apostolic" church of Christ. Our claim to be an embodiment of the church of Christ does not rest on a short list of the characteristics that distinguishes us from other traditions. Overwhelmingly, it rests on what we hold in common with them!

Nevertheless, the Church of Christ does have some distinguishing characteristics. Or at least we like to think we do. And yet I am not sure that we possess any belief about faith and order that is utterly unique to us. What about baptism for "the remission of sins?" The Orthodox and Roman Catholics never abandoned this teaching. What about a capella music? The Orthodox and many Protestant groups sing without instrumental accompaniment. What about the frequent observance of the Lord's Supper? The Roman Catholics and Orthodox celebrate it more often that we do. What about preaching, teaching, repentance, and reverence for Scripture? No, these are common aspects of nearly all traditions. Are our distinctive features found in what we reject—creeds and extra congregational authorities? No. There are also traditions that reject these things. What then is unique about us? What gives the Church of Christ its unique identity?

In answering these questions, allow me to remind you of what I said at the beginning of this section: the Church of Christ is a tradition sustained and animated by devotion to a set of interlocking ideas. It is not the ideas themselves, considered separately, that give this tradition its unique identity. It is the particular combination and ordering of these ideas. And the particular combination and ordering of these ideas were determined by the religious situation in 19th century America, by the personalities of its earliest pioneers, by its internal and external debates, and by the steady stream of leaders that have articulated the meaning of the tradition to its members. The identity of the tradition is also determined by its institutions—colleges, newspapers, journals and publishing houses, lectureships, seminars, local preachers' meetings, and the vast informal networks of friends. The bottom line is that traditions are kept alive by communication. When the leaders and most members of a congregation cease to communicate with others in the tradition and cease to be devoted to the interlocking set of ideas that gives the Church of Christ its identity, it ceases to be a Church of Christ even if it retains the name.

I Stayed for the Light

Do I have theological reasons for remaining in Churches of Christ? Yes, I do. I really believe those ideas that we have combined and ordered in our own unique way. And I believe that our ordering of those ideas preserves things that ought to be preserved and embodied in the world. I am fully and painfully aware that we have not always lived up to the ideals that inspired my admiration: simplicity, rationality, order, Scriptural authority, the normativity of New Testament Christianity, desire for unity with other believers, and so many more. I affirm our exclusive use of a capella singing in worship as worth preserving. I treasure our view that baptism and the Lord's Supper are more than mere human responses to God's historical actions on our behalf but also involve God's action on our behalf in the performance of them.

I shall conclude by quoting the famous words of Daniel Webster uttered before the Supreme Court of the United States on March 10, 1818, in defense of Dartmouth College against the State of New Hampshire. The legislature had passed a law declaring Dartmouth a public institution. In his speech, Webster pled,

> Sir, you may destroy this little institution; it is weak, it is in your hands! I know it is one of the lesser lights in the literary horizon of our country. You may put it out! But if you do so, you must carry through your work! You must extinguish, one after another, all those great lights of science which for more than a century have thrown their radiance over our land! It is, Sir, as I have said, a small college. And yet *there are those who love it!*[2]

The Church of Christ is a little thing, I know. *But there are those who love it*. Perhaps it is a "lesser light." But I shall not be the one to put it out.

---

[2] Kenneth E. Shewmaker, *"The Completest Man" Documents from the Papers of Daniel Webster* (Hanover, NH: Dartmouth University Press of New England, 1990), pp. 168-169.

I Stayed to Bloom Where I Am Planted

John Wilson[1]

Two points are necessary for full disclosure. First, I have always been rather attracted to the greeting card admonition to "bloom where you are planted," or, in its Pauline permutation, "let each of you remain in the condition in which you were called," (I Cor. 7:20). I realize that this adage represents a point of view not appealing or even an option to everyone and so I embrace it in a very non-judgmental way—while at the same time seeking to understand those who feel differently. The Churches of Christ have been an overwhelmingly positive force in my life. They have done me a great deal of good and very little harm. They have not been responsible for career failures, or personal relationship failures, or emotional damages of various kinds; I have managed to initiate and nourish enough of these sorts of things on my own without requiring ecclesiastical assistance. The Churches of Christ did not get me fired, overly exasperated, or personally humiliated; nor did they impede me in reaching out for my life-goals. On the contrary, they

---

[1] John Wilson was educated at Harding University and the University of Iowa (Ph.D.). He currently serves as Professor of Religion, Emeritus, Seaver College and Director Emeritus, Institute for the Study of Archaeology and Religion, Seaver College, Pepperdine University. He is also Project Director, Banias (Israel) Archaeological Project and has excavated at Capernaum and Jerusalem in Israel. He has numerous appearances on radio and television and hundreds of lectures throughout the world, writer of many radio and television scripts. Among his published works are *Religion: A Preface* and *Caesarea Philippi: Banias, the Last City of Pan*, and more.

have done me great good. They furnished the impetus for a love of education and learning; they provided me an exciting and fulfilling career path; they furnished the foundation for an immense and loving family (both spiritual and genetic) as a child, father, and grandfather. Within their bounds were dug and maintained the wells from which I have drawn my sense of identity and purpose.

I repeat that I am well aware that not everyone has been dealt this sort of hand, and thus my inclination not to judge the actions or opinions of others on this point. I suppose if pressed to do so I could make a list of affronts, deprecations, obstacles, misplaced values and annoying bits of inherited misinformation associated in some way with the Churches of Christ which have accompanied my otherwise rather smooth ride. I have never seen any particular usefulness in keeping track of these sorts of things, however. I am, I think, as aware of them as the next person. I have had decades to contemplate both the strengths and foibles of my spiritual forebears and contemporary associates. I was fortunate to grow up in a home where strengths and foibles alike were frankly acknowledged and thus discovering them furnished no particular surprises, shook no foundations, and certainly required no radical reactions one way or the other. Rather, as I gradually learned to recognize the idiosyncrasies, inconsistencies and occasional fumbling, my reaction has tended to be simply, *c'est la vie—what else is new?*

Peter and Paul both call the Church a family (Gal 6:10; I Pet 2:17; 5:9) and I have taken that analogy seriously. I realize we can't simply transfer this magnificent theological figure lock, stock, and barrel to the entity that historians might call the "Churches of Christ—A Cappella", but I think it has a valuable function nevertheless. Some people are tragically abandoned or repudiated by their families and spend their lives searching (alas, often in vain) for a fulfilling substitute. Others begin to dwell on the often very real flaws and failures of the family which produced and nurtured them and leave of their own free will, sometimes in a huff, searching for Utopia. In the biological realm, we usually consider this outcome a tragedy and a deviation from the intended nature of things. These people often seem to us tragic figures, trying to find themselves a seat at someone else's family table. They fancy that in this new family there will be none of the flaws and failures they have found so loathsome in their own. They may be led to this romantic conclusion because they believe that the faults of *their* family were unique to it and that it is uniquely unable to furnish them the succor and protection they long to have. Sadly, experience may eventually teach them that the source of the problem was not in the unique failures of the family from whence they came, but rather had something more to do with the universal frailty of all human endeavors.

I have had the opportunity to interact on a warm and friendly basis with fellow-travelers from many spiritual families, some quite different from my own—within the larger Christian world and even among the plethora of "world religions." I don't recall a single instance when those who had chosen to invest their lives, eyes wide open, in the spiritual family into which they were born, were at the same time unable or unwilling to see its foibles as well as its strengths. And only a few of these people found their sanguine assessment to be an unconquerable obstacle. For various reasons, I do not number myself among this later minority.

Some have been given the comforting ability to see the flaws in their parents and their siblings but nevertheless to continue to love them and feel a deep responsibility for their well-being. In biological families, this course of action is seen as a normal expectation and at the same time somewhat heroic. Such persons may from time to time have had an urge to flee, but this feeling soon passed. Instead of resorting to flight they decided to bloom where they were planted. Their prayer borrowed its marrow from the saintly Francis of Assisi: where there was hatred, they were inclined to react by trying to sow love; where there was injury, pardon; where there was darkness, light. They sought not so much to be consoled as to console, to be understood as to understand; to be loved as to love. It is a kind of loyalty which sometimes borders on folly, I know, but also on nobility. I have often heard the voice of old Polycarp, Bishop of Smyrna, speaking to me from both my inner being and from the mists of history. Called under threat of death itself to abandon the cause for which he had lived, he could not leave that which he had served for so long and which in his forgiving heart and memory had never done him any wrong. Well done, old Polycarp!

The second point of full disclosure has to do with my understanding of what the Churches of Christ-A Cappella essentially *are* and how they fit into the larger scheme of things. Jesus' message was about the Kingdom of God (Mark 1:15). Those are two enormous words: Kingdom and God. They are words which should be understood alongside the awesome images provided to us by modern astronomers, images which have shown us a Universe immensely more expansive than we have ever heretofore dreamed. If God rules the Universe, it is this Hubble-revealed Universe that He rules: worlds beyond our ability to number, space beyond our ability to measure, time beyond all imagining. If He has a Kingdom, it extends even to those far reaches still beyond our ability to see, and far too complex and far-away for even a space telescope to catch its limits in some net of light. And even on this tiny globe where we live, dangling like a minuscule speck of dust in the enormity of space, His Kingdom can hardly be imagined to consist entirely of a rather small group of people camped around an imaginary line running through the American heartlands for the last couple of centuries. Nor, for that matter, can it be some sort of World Council of Churches—however diverse and inclusive. More than a half-century ago J.B. Phillips warned us, "Your God is Too Small." To which we must add, ". . . and so may be our estimate of His Kingdom."

But freely conceding to this undeniable (at least to me) recognition provides no compelling rationale for separating ourselves from our spiritual heritage—be it ever so humble. On the contrary, it allows us to take comfort in the fact that God's Kingdom is so comprehensive, so diverse and variegated, that even *we* are a part of it, that we have our own duties to perform, that it is not ours to say, when we look at the complexity of the Kingdom, "but Lord, what about them?" Rather, we hear the words of the Teacher, "What is that to you? You must follow me!" (John 21:22). When with Isaiah we are inclined to see ourselves only as people of unclean lips, dwelling in the midst of a people of unclean lips, we take comfort in the fact that it was directly to such a one as this, among such a people as this, that the mighty temple voice cried out, "Who will go for us?" Bloom where you are planted.

"But," you say, "is not your choice simply an appeal to inertia? Of course, it is always easier to stay put. And if everyone thought in this way, the world would never change." The point is a reasonable one and carries some weight. But as I have sought to find the essence of our movement, behind the bluster or prejudices or oversimplifications or regional naivety or imposed artificial structures, I have found good, even exciting, reasons to contribute to the coming of the Kingdom right here—where I was planted.

Because it is so immense and so complex, God's Kingdom has always required a "host of witnesses" (Heb. 12:1). Some of these have witnessed to one aspect of the whole and others to another. There is no reason to be discomforted by this fact. Some have given the biblical word for witness its most special meaning—martyrdom. Their message has been that some things are more valuable than life itself. Some have insisted on taking the words of Jesus about turning the other cheek quiet literally, and have turned their backs on all violence whatsoever. Some have literally done what Jesus advised the rich young ruler to do, and given all they had to the poor. Some have devoted their lives and energy to a better understanding of the Scriptures, or to translating them into other languages, or to lives dedicated entirely to the proclamation of the Gospel, or to feeding the hungry. And as often as not, these forms of witness have had their corporate expressions. They have been especially practiced not simply by individuals with a special sense of calling, but by whole movements. Often the call to witness is not so much the lonely one heard by Isaiah in the temple of God (Isa. 6:8) as it is a call for "us" (Isa. 49:6) corporately to witness in some perhaps small but nevertheless significant way as a fragment of the larger light.

Can we find the way to our own particular kind of witness in the strengths of our own heritage, and make those strengths our witness, rather than drearily picking away at the scabs and sores? Is it possible to make what is distinctive about us a way to form our witness, instead of some sort of obstacle in our way? Not every disciple has died for his or her faith; not every disciple has sold everything and given it to the poor. But I am glad that some have—and in so doing have taught me things about the Kingdom I could not have learned so well otherwise. These saints witness to a truth the rest of us might otherwise be inclined to overlook. Might we find a way to do the same?

Some, on discovering that the impact of Jesus of Nazareth on our world and its history has been much greater and more complex than they thought (a discovery often associated with going to graduate school, or moving to another county, for example), have become ashamed of the distinctives of their own Kingdom-corner. They have come to feel (for reasons that seem mysterious to me) that abandoning these distinctives, and even ridiculing them, will help them blend into the larger world they have discovered. Maybe, by such means, they will get into that exclusive club of which so many of those they have come to know in the larger world seem to be members. Our distinctives seem to such people, at this stage in their journey of self-discovery, to be vestiges of their rural, ignorant, hillbilly origins. They will struggle mightily to get rid of such embarrassments.

"You are not one of those Church of Christers, are you?"

"I am not; I am not; I am not!"

But it may be that others, perhaps taking a few more graduate courses, reading a few more books, and visiting a few more exotic places, eventually discover instead that the distinctives which have characterized the Churches of Christ are mostly perfectly legitimate points of view which have been held, defended and perpetrated by some of the great minds and movements of Christendom, in some cases for centuries. And in some cases, these distinctive perspectives and understandings have gotten lost in the swirling mists of modern religion. They seek for those who will give them a voice in our own day. For such perspectives and understandings the cry goes out, "Whom shall we send, and who will go for us?" Answering this call is a legitimate and sometimes even noble task—blooming where you are planted.

But to what are we called to bear witness? How and where may we find in the soil of our heritage the nutrients which might feed the mighty Kingdom of God? Not the only witnesses, perhaps, or the most eloquent—but witnesses nevertheless? I suggest at least the following six.

1. Reason as the Path to Knowing
2. Restoration as the Means for Cleansing Change
3. Corporate and Local Leadership as the Protector of Spiritual Freedom

4. Communal Worship from the Inside Out
5. Baptism and Communion as Sacrament and Symbol
6. Fellowship, Benevolence and Proclamation as Central Tasks

Reason as the Path to Knowing

The Churches of Christ have been accused of having "head religion" instead of "heart religion." Strictly speaking, the charge is historically unfair—but never mind. There is no shame in calling for a return to the use of that faculty which is at the center of the capacity to be human—to think, to work toward logical conclusions, to have reasons for our feelings. At this point in the evolution of human society one would think it unnecessary to bring special attention to the fact that feelings, even religious feelings, if generated from nothing deeper than momentary sensations, can result in an existential tossing to and fro, a tragic sense of betrayal when found to be in error, and sometimes even a justification for that which is most dark and sinister within us. But in a Post-Modern Age, when all things are justified by the prompting of the emotions, and where one's feeling becomes one's truth, Reason, like Wisdom her sister, "shouts in the streets."

> She cries out in the public square.
> She calls to the crowds along the main street,
> To those gathered in front of the city gate;
> How long, you simpletons,
> Will you insist on being simpleminded?
> How long will you mockers relish your mocking?
> How long will you fools hate knowledge?
> Come and listen to my counsel.
> I'll share my heart with you
> And make you wise. (Proverbs 1:20-23)

Our spiritual forefathers often preached from the text "Come now, let us reason together" (Isaiah 1:18). This invitation is part of our gift to the larger world. I delight in serving the cause of reason and find in it no cause for shame or abandonment.

Restoration as the Means for Cleansing Change

We are not the first to urge the Church to cleanse itself by returning to its origins. But we have been particularly diligent in calling for "restoration." I am well aware of our inconsistencies and ham-handedness in achieving this goal. Nevertheless I believe that history has taught us that the Church, if not called with a certain abruptness and persistence to return to its origins, tends to drift into actions and take on ideas which would be abhorrent to him who came crying out "Repent, for the Kingdom of God is at hand." And for those who, looking upon that one and hearing his voice, believe they are seeing and hearing the Eternal Father, it is good to be with those who call for a return to the shores of First Century Galilee to right our wandering course. We do not have to be legalists or bibliolaters to accept that those who were closest to him, and have left their record of his life and voice, have a place in his cause which is *sui generis*. Their witness is a special witness. It is in this sense that we remain "Bible Centered" and thus in constant labor to draw ourselves and our fellow-believers back into the simple yet revolutionary vortex of his message. There is no shame, or even any exclusive historical insight, in "speaking where the Bible speaks and being silent where the Bible is silent." In such a simple idea there lies the fuel which burns away the dross which has over and over again hidden what should have been the Light of the World. The soil in which our heritage in the Churches of Christ is planted was in its essence not reactionary, as some might claim. Rather, it is revolutionary. It witnesses to the paradox—that the surest course toward change involves a return to the beginnings. It is never popular to be a critic, of course. It is always safer and less stressful to accept the status quo. But the more satisfied Christendom becomes with itself, the more relevant and urgent our witness. At their center, prophets are restorationists. There is no shame in joining them.

> "If you will return, O Israel," declares the LORD, "Then you should return to Me. And if you will put away your detested things from My presence, And will not waver, And you will swear, 'As the LORD lives,' In truth, in justice and in righteousness; Then the nations will bless themselves in Him, And in Him they will glory." (Jeremiah 4:1-2)

Corporate and Local Leadership as the Protector of Spiritual Freedom

Nowadays "church order" seems a hopelessly pedantic subject. What possible difference can it make how Jesus' disciples organize themselves? I am happy to remain among those who believe it does make a difference. The Church has for centuries wandered off its course at the instigation of those who thought of themselves as "pillars;" loving "to be greeted with respect in the marketplaces and to be called 'Rabbi'"; disciples of Diotrephes who "love to be first." It is good to be among those who resist the recurring tendency for one person, however well-intentioned, to be "the pastor" and dominate the community of brothers and sisters. It is good to be among those who resist those increasingly powerful bureaucracies created by gatherings of such persons who then seek to dominate those with whom they never physically sit at the Lord's Table. Our weapon of resistance is "congregational autonomy." What chaos have such bureaucracies visited upon what should have been a simple life of Kingdom fellowship! How satisfying to be able to refuse to submit to them!

Communal Worship from the Inside Out

The New Testament says little about corporate worship, and almost nothing about music, but in recent times these rather peripheral matters seem to be the center of attention in many quarters. People actually chose their church on the basis of how well they like the praise band (or the presence or absence thereof), or what they "get" from the public "services." I like to think of myself as something of an aesthete, musically and otherwise. Nevertheless, when it comes to aesthetic beauty, I am happy to accept that "the earth is the Lord's and the fullness thereof"—and thus does "all nature sing, and 'round us rings the music of the spheres"—but that the Family of God which represents his Kingdom needs in its communal life only the simplest kinds of spiritual expression. The profoundest worship, like the truest ethical behavior, originates in the heart, not in the ears—and not on the stage.

Jesus explained that concept definitively to the Samaritan woman at the well in answering her "worship question," and again in the Sermon on the Mount. What evidence we have suggests that the earliest Christians understood this dominical answer to the woman to apply to their meetings together. And if there was music in their simple meetings (maybe a bit of singing together "after supper"?), it was the symphony created as the believers each played on the harp of her or his heart. This is the consistent figure used by the New Testament writers and the earliest Christians. These instruments were conveniently located in the same internal fountainhead from which all their truly significant behaviors and character poured forth. Both worship and Kingdom ethics originated there and proceeded from the inside out. We are not the first, nor will we be the last, to bring this witness to the light. But it is, for us and them, a meaningful and significant witness.

Baptism and Communion as Sacrament and Symbol

In an age when the historic "ordinances" of the Christian faith are being progressively shunted aside and trivialized, it is satisfying to continue to witness to their centrality and to their power. Witnesses are needed to demonstrate the immensely effective symbolism found in the ritual of total immersion of a human being who is capable of believing and confessing the Lordship of Jesus; and at the same time, to remain true to the understanding which has been shared by the vast majority of believers throughout the millennia—that this act is not simply a symbol, but also an act of covenant which marks the crossing of a firm border between the world and the kingdom. And if we have not yet quite recaptured the table-practice of the earliest believers, we have at least called attention to the centrality of a family meal as a real, and not merely a symbolic portal into the presence of Jesus where "two or three are gathered in his name."

Fellowship, Benevolence, and Proclamation as Central Tasks

And finally, partly because of the very simplicity of the things I have listed above, we are able to witness to the central tasks which the Teacher laid out as the agenda for those who sought to follow him into the Kingdom. Set free from the complexities of bureaucracy and political maneuvering, liberated from ecclesiastical autocracy, freed from the pretensions of musicians, orators, and showmen of various kinds who somehow tend to confuse the work of the Kingdom with their performances—we have been called to witness to truths easily lost in the foggy world of contemporary "religion." We can declare that "Church" is not an event which we observe as spectators, or a complex institution demanding our time and resources, but rather a family of brothers and sisters in fellowship. We can keep it very simple, as did the Teacher: feed the poor, clothe the naked, honor and participate in the community of faith, proclaim the Kingdom, live by its ethic of the heart.

I find it possible (albeit very imperfectly) to witness to all these things, and respond to all these challenges, and at the same time remain among those who have provided me the spiritual food without which I would have surely fainted along the way. And so—I will continue to seek to bloom where I have been planted.

I Stayed for the Inheritance

Chris Rosser[1]

The following is not an academic essay; it is my report of an unusual experience of hearing voices in a library archives. In relation to the question of *Why I stayed?*, it was while pondering this conundrum in the quiet space of the archives that I began to hear them, whispering, and to sense them, watching. As a librarian of the meaner sort, I am not much given to flights of fancy or spooky rumor; yet, I cannot deny the experience and even now must ask myself why I stayed in the archive after the first sensation of *other presences* prickled my skin and induced sudden pallor. Had I fled as both instinct and sanity demanded—but wait: let me offer explanation at the start so that sense can be made of the ending.

I am a Campbellite, born and bred in the Churches of Christ. The worst of us believe in ghosts. We believe in the Bible and in our capacity to discern evident truths, to divide essentials from the rest of it. Such is my inheritance as a son of Stone-Campbell. I was raised in a fundamentalist home, swaddled by the rhetoric of exclusivity and exceptionalism;[2] yet as flies have their way with a decomposing thing, so questions frustrated and buzzed about, rendering me first numb and then nearly dead to Restorationists'

---

[1] Chris Rosser serves as Theological Librarian for the Beam Library at Oklahoma Christian University. Before completing an MLIS and MDiv, he and his family worked as missionaries in Japan and ministered in Oklahoma City area Churches of Christ.

[2] Language like this depicts my own, early experience in Churches of Christ. I do not intend unwarranted caricature, but my assumption is that others questioning whether or not to stay have had similar experiences.

pleas. They wanted brains, not blood; at least, such was my perception, and I moved among them as missionary and minister in conservative congregations, posturing as a committed Campbellite, concocting strategies for escape. Yet at present I serve as librarian at a Churches of Christ university, with access to Stone-Campbell archives—a windowless, sterile, climate-controlled space with thick, blue carpet; flickering fluorescents spattering glow upon rows of shelves of fusty, old books and pamphlets; with a growling dehumidifier and the stale breath of sleeping tomes—to this archive I now return.

Perched on a hardback, behind a low desk, buried in the archives, I had crafted my thesis—*critique is Campbellite patrimony; prophetic criticism is a harbinger of restoration*—when I began to experience the unsettling sense that someone was watching me. Turning, I discovered no one, save a reprint portrait of Alexander Campbell framed and tacked to an otherwise vacant wall. He looked grim and ungenerous, yet I did not find fault; poor soul, he had been painted that way. I returned to my thesis.

Concise, yet wordy; too thick to be profitable. The thought came like words from behind me, though I cannot be sure that anyone actually spoke. Nevertheless, I leaped from the hardback and spun on my assailant, fists wielding sharpened pencils. "Who's there?" I demanded; no one was there. Campbell's portrait bored holes through me. Surely, dear reader, you are preparing yourself for what must happen next: Campbell's ghost or some similar apparition floats through the wall and rebuffs me like Scrooge's Marley. As a librarian familiar with such tales, I also assumed as much and acted preemptively: "You're one to criticize thick writing, aren't you, Mr. Campbell?" I squeaked. In retrospect, I am grateful no colleagues overheard this one-sided conversation. Campbell said nothing; he continued to stare with furrowed brow. Worrying that I had upset him, I calmed myself and tried to explain.

"You see, I am trying to think of good reasons why I stayed with the Churches of Christ. Actually, this is a difficult question. I wrestle with the church: we've not been fair with Scripture, and we've been unkind to others, in my opinion." I spoke furtively, wondering how he might react. He remained silent, so I continued: "I'm not sure I have a reasoned explanation for why I stayed. I have a poem and a thought if you'd like to hear them?" Here, he seemed to me mildly intrigued, though his expression hardly changed. Like a child, I felt eager to impress, so I began to share with his portrait my experiences as a missionary in Mito, Japan. I told him about a Japanese man, an artist, and poet, who began his career as a physical education instructor at a junior high school. On the first day of classes, he decided to demonstrate his athletic prowess for a group of eager students; he back-flipped off a table, landed on his neck, and became an instant quadriplegic. From that moment on, Tomihiro Hoshino was confined to a bed, fully relying on others for sustenance and care. Believing himself incurably diminished, he attempted to take his own life. However, he encountered a Christian whose message of hope resurrected joy.

Tomihiro learned to paint with a brush between his teeth; now, he has become famous throughout Japan for simple yet inspiring illustrations of nature coupled with the powerful words of his poetry. I myself was struck by one poem in particular: beside a watercolor willow, the poet writes, "A tree rises forth from the mud of its birth but spreads its branches wide."[3] For me, his poem teaches a profound lesson in ecclesiology: I was born into a particular faith-heritage, an inheritance passed down from many generations, yet I also might enjoy near boundless opportunity to learn of Christ from others, provided I am humble and desirous of dialogue. Like a tree, I rise up out of the soil of my Restoration heritage; like a tree, I spread wide my branches to gather more light.

So I looked Campbell dead in the eye and proclaimed, "We flourish in the reaching, the stretching, the recognition of our interdependency, and in a desire to connect with others; we wither otherwise. I am committed to the preservation of my fellowship, but my fellowship is not a source of all light." I tried to be eloquent, but he seemed unimpressed. Rustling leaves on a nearby shelf distracted us as a yellowed tome opened, suspended in air, pages flipping as if by an unseen, impatient hand. Then began the whispering; or rather, I seemed to now discern voices that had all along been gossiping. The floating book offered a delicate "ahem" and whispered:

---

[3] From an inspiring poem by Japanese Christian Tomihiro Hoshino, *Journey of the Wind* (Tōkyō: *Rippū Shobō, 1988), 48-49.

> I should have mentioned that some of the evergreens are nearly one hundred feet high, and still in fine vigor. Within the yard, along the fence, is a pleasant little walk, shaded by large Ailantus, or the "tree of heaven." It lies on the road to the winding Buffalo Creek. At the end of the walk was a beautiful little arbor, covered with Virginia creeper and woodbine. It was called "The Lovers' Retreat," and in it many an impressive sigh was breathed that betokened more than words. Near to the arbor stood a lofty linden tree—greatly admired by Mr. Campbell. Around its base a seat encircled it; all of which gave enchantment to the spot, of which now only wrecks are left.[4]

"What?" I asked, rightly perplexed. "What do you mean?"

"She wants you to know that her husband, Mr. Campbell, was quite fond of trees and shrubbery. Also, that he once enjoyed a 'Lovers' Retreat' and there sighed impressive sighs." A voice from the curio cabinet now spoke: his was not a whisper; it was a tinny resonance with a Scottish accent. The voice belonged to a pewter chalice, turned on end: two plates like round, saucer eyes, the chalice handle a high, stately nose, and a thin crack in the cup articulated unexpected speech. "Selina's his widow, and she's politely talking trees with you, since you seem to like them as well, not knowing what else to say, it being difficult to follow your story about a crippled man and mud. You're a bit thick, then, aren't you?" Here was a lovely, old communion set.

As I examined the cup and two dishes,[5] their worn edges, dents and creases proclaiming years of use, the discolored places where countless hands had partaken, sipped, and passed, it occurred to me that these precious objects had once been bearers of our Lord's body and blood. Yet now, such honorable Christ-bearing vessels were retired, shelved in the library, displayed as relics bereft of their

---

[4] Excerpt from Selina Huntington Campbell, *Home Life and Reminiscences of Alexander Campbell* (St. Louis: J. Burns, 1882), 53-54.

[5] Dr. Lynn McMillon donated to the library an old, pewter communion set he acquired from a Glasite congregation in Edinburgh. The set is displayed in a special cabinet in the Restoration Movement History archives, Oklahoma Christian University. Glasite and Sandemanian congregations represent back-to-the-Bible movements that form a backdrop to the American Restoration Movement. Remarkably, these are Christian groups for which there is a clear beginning and ending of their movement.

Host, a memory of words that had been their gift and burden, *This do in remembrance of Me*. A similar sentiment seemed to be on his mind as well: "Oh, Alex, we're quite a pair, we two, shelved in a library, forevermore! Once bearers of supernal mystery, now shelved and suspended: I in my glass-paned casket, and you strung up by your shoulders, pinned to a wall! Lord help us, it's a cruel end." Campbell's brow remained furrowed and his gaze fixed. I shrugged at the chalice. "Ah, it's no better for you," he remarked. "Minister and missionary are titles worn with valor; *librarian* is best worn with a cardigan!" I shifted the subject.

"Campbell hanging there surprises me; I assumed he would fearsomely emerge from his portrait as Vachel Lindsay prophesied, turning the hearts of renegade Campbellites back to their primitive roots. Do you know Lindsay's poem?" Here I began to recite:

> And we glanced at the portrait of that most benign of men
> Looking down through the evening gleam . . . .
> For once upon a time . . .
> Long, long ago . . .
> In the holy forest land
> There was a jolly pre-millennial band,
> When that text-armed apostle, Alexander Campbell
> Held deathless debate with the wicked "infi-del."
> The clearing was a picnic ground.
> Squirrels were barking.
> The seventeen year locust charged by.
> Wild turkeys perched on high.
> And millions of wild pigeons
> Broke the limbs of trees,
> Then shut out the sun, as they swept on their way.
> But ah, the wilder dove of God flew down
> To bring a secret glory, and to stay,
> With the proud hunter-trappers, patriarchs that came
> To break bread together and to pray
> And oh the music of each living throbbing thing
> When Campbell arose,

A pillar of fire,
The great high priest of Spring. [6]

The archive was a tomb again. Whispering had silenced; yet I sensed a latent energy, increasing like dawn's light spreading her blanket over a sleepy forest, beckoning wakeful night-creatures to bed, so this energy seemed to me a kind of dark light rising to wake hushed, sleepy things, and with explosive sound books flew from shelves, flapping like birds, rustling leaves, roosting and perching; pamphlets were barking; periodicals folded themselves origami-style into buzzing things; I pressed myself down into the hardback as millions of index cards erupted from a card-catalogue morgue, twisting, bending, becoming paper cranes. All was commotion, a clutter of sound and sight so inappropriate to the archive I was beside myself with emotion. Then came Campbell, rousing himself from his portrait to address the gathered:

"And lo! ye shall bind the judgments of men, (and more especially of women,) as with a band of iron; and ye shall make them blind in the midst of light, even as the owl is blind in the noon day sun, and behold ye shall lead them captive to your reverend wills."[7]

---

[6] Vachel Lindsay (1879-1931) was a celebrated American poet and "stout Campbellite" who is best known for his poems "The Congo" (inspired by a Disciples missionary) and "Abraham Lincoln Walks at Midnight." For his complete poem about Campbell, see Vachel Lindsay, "Alexander Campbell," in *The Golden Whales of California* (New York: MacMillan, 1920): 171-181. A brief description of Lindsay can be found in Charles R. Gresham, "Lindsay, Vachel," in *Encyclopedia of the Stone-Campbell Movement*, edited by Douglas Foster, et al., 479-480 (Grand Rapids, MI: William B. Eerdmans, 2004). For more on Lindsay's association with the Stone-Campbell heritage, see, William Frederic Rothenburger, "Vachel Lindsay," *Shane Quarterly* 5, no. 2-3 (April 1944): 144-147; and see especially Olive Lindsay Wakefield, "Vachel Lindsay, Disciple," *Shane Quarterly* 5, no. 2-3 (April 1944): 82-107. In the house of Lindsay's grandfather, famed Disciples preacher Ephraim Frazee, "The haloed head of Alexander Campbell looked down upon us from above the fireplace, and rows of calf-bound *Millennial Harbingers* stood out impressively on the crowded bookcase shelves" (Wakefield, 102).

[7] See his wonderfully satirical rebuke of the dominant culture of church leadership in Alexander Campbell, "The Third Epistle of Peter: To the Preachers and Rulers of Congregations," *The Christian Baptist* 2, no. 12 (July 1825): 243-247.

"Preach! Prophesy! Preach!" they shouted music, a paper chorale, a score of living, throbbing things. The archive had become a picnic ground strewn with folio and leaflet.

"Teach them to believe that you have the care of their souls, and that the saving mysteries are for your explaining; and when you explain your *mysteries*, encompass them round about with words as with a bright veil, so bright that through it no man can see."[8] His voice was a thunder, magniloquent harbinger of sweet spring rain. "Preach! Prophesy! Preach!" Again the chorus sang, and I could feel night descending upon the archive as swiftly as day had engulfed us moments before. Against the settling dusk, Campbell called for hush and offered an impressive sigh:

The present material universe, yet unrevealed in all its area, in all its tenantries, in all its riches, beauty and grandeur, will be wholly regenerated. Of this fact we have full assurance: since he that now sits upon the Throne of the Universe, has pledged his word for it, saying, "*Behold, I will create all things new*;" —consequently "new heavens, new earth," —consequently, new tenantries, new employments, new pleasures, new joys, new ecstasies. There is a fullness of joy, a fullness of glory, and a fullness of blessedness, of which no living man, however enlightened, however enlarged, however gifted, ever formed or entertained one adequate conception.[9]

The humidifier growled. Night had completely come upon us, which I sensed despite the constant buzzy flickering of fluorescents above. As one who dreams, I voiced an elegy, cold and strong:

I have begun to count my dead.
They wave green branches
Around my head,
Put their hands upon my shoulders,
Stand behind me,

---

[8] Ibid., 246.

[9] From Campbell's final contribution to the Millennial Harbinger, published only a few short months before his death in March, 1866. See Alexander Campbell, "The Gospel," *Millennial Harbinger* 36, no. 11 (November 1865): 516-517. Vachel Lindsay includes this excerpt as preface to his poem "Alexander Campbell."

Fly above me –
Presences that love me.[10]

"*He* is here, you know," the chalice whispered. "Here, but over there." His saucer eyes directed me to an adjacent wall; but there, what I knew to be rows of large, gray archival boxes had grotesquely transformed, appearing to my senses as the large, metallic drawers one finds in a morgue. A paper crane brushed me in flight to a particular compartment and rested upon the handle. I approached (how could I do otherwise?), grasped the handle, and pulled the creaking drawer until its table had fully extended, its singular content fully exposed. Long, white cloth covered a corpse; I pulled it back to reveal the face and torso of Vachel Lindsay, Disciples poet, troubadour tramp, Preacher of the gospel of beauty who beheld "millennial trumpets poised, half-lifted, millennial trumpets that wait."[11] His expression was of one who sleeps, though his body was cold and stiff, and his tweed suit smelled of mothballs. Chalice broke out a melancholy tune: *I know an old poet who swallowed the Ly…* Somehow, his lyric was not inappropriate to the moment. Whimsy lay curled like a sleeping cat at the corners of Lindsay's mouth and eyes. He was lovely to behold, as if at any moment Restoration might overcome his repose.

---

[10] Lindsay, 174.

[11] Lindsay, 175. Let me offer a brief word about Vachel Lindsay, who was raised and remained a committed Campbellite. Indeed, he shared Campbell's vision for America: that God was bringing civic and spiritual revival through the restoration of primitive Christianity, that light from America would become hope for the world. Lindsay was a troubadour poet, wandering the nation, trading songs for food and a night's lodging. His poetry itself embodied a mission to recall increasingly secularized and materialistic Americans to simpler life and civic renewal. As mentioned, Lindsay became an acclaimed American poet; yet figuratively, "he felt compelled to take Alexander Campbell with him while he carried out his mission" (Masters, 299). But his mission was failing; America was not living out the ideal either Campbell or Lindsay envisioned. Recognition that his message—his prophetic critique of modern, urban, industrial society—was largely unheeded "caused him deep sorrow and loneliness and, eventually, real depression. Like many another seer, he was speaking in an unknown tongue" (Wakefield, 82). On December 5, 1931, Lindsay took his own life by ingesting Lysol. See Edgar Lee Masters, *Vachel Lindsay: A Poet in America* (New York: Biblo and Tannen, 1969); Jeffrey Folks, "Vachel Lindsay's Covenant with America," *Modern Age* 50, no. 4 (Fall 2008): 321-331.

Though in whispers now, the chorus of books, pamphlets, leaflets, periodicals, index cards, and archival miscellany resumed their music: "Preach. Prophesy. Preach. Open his mouth, librarian." Both hands reaching, I lightly grasped his forehead with my left and gently pressed upon his chin with my right. His mouth stiffly opened, revealing behind his top teeth a folded scrap of parchment neatly stuck to the roof of his mouth. I confess to employing a nearby staple-puller to fish it out. Once in hand, I unfolded the scrap and read aloud:

> I come to you from Campbell,
> Turn again, prodigal
> Haunted by his name!
> Artist, singer, builder,
> The forest's son or daughter!
> You, the blasphemer
> Will yet know repentance,
> And Campbell old and grey
> Will lead you to the dream-side
> Of a pennyroyal river.
> While your proud heart is shaken
> Your confession will be taken
> And your sins baptized away.[12]

Then, I discerned beating, as of a human heart. *Could it be?* I wondered. *Is Restoration at hand?* As the beating grew louder I recognized it as a pounding, clanking, hammering, as of iron striking iron. Turning from Lindsay's corpse I beheld a great anvil, and upon the anvil, a book bound in iron, and the book was the history of the Stone-Campbell Movement, a capture of lives intersecting, ideas erupting, sin, pain, weddings, funerals, and beauty like a widow's smile. A host of smiths, women, and men, were hammering, working bellows, dousing hot metal so that steam hissed and rose in serpentine curls. "What is this?" I asked? "They are Prophets and Priests," answered Chalice. "One hardens and sets the bind; the other makes it molten and malleable. Both are necessary, but their blows are a dance: many, many awkward missteps."

"Was Lindsay Prophet or Priest?"

---

[12] Lindsay, 180.

"Prophet."

"And Campbell?"

"Campbell was both Prophet and Priest, binding and loosing, binding and loosing; it was all a great negotiation, you know."

"And what should I be then, Prophet or Priest?"

"Both. Neither. You be *archivist*; help remind us of things we'd forgot, will you?"

One of the smiths then smashed his thumb, and there was no end of loud cursing. I found my hardback and seated myself at the low desk, returning to my thesis. Campbell was right: *Concise, yet wordy; too thick to be profitable.* I could feel the archive returning to its earlier, sterile condition: papers fluttered and flitted about, books re-shelved, Lindsay's drawer shut, the anvil was put away, and a wall of archival boxes replaced my impression of a morgue. I let go an impressive sigh.

Chalice rolled his saucer eyes at me. "Back to work? We've not finished! Alex was wondering about your thought."

"My thought?"

"Yes, *thought*. Earlier you said you had a poem and a thought. You shared the muddy poem; why not share the bloody thought?" At this, I suddenly grew very sleepy and desired nothing but to rest my head upon the low desk and be lulled into oblivion by the growling humidifier. "Preach, prophesy, preach," he whispered. "Preach, prophesy, preach." I stirred myself, glancing up at Campbell's portrait, who furrowed his brow.

"A poem and a thought?" I asked.

"And a thick thesis!" replied Chalice.

"*Critique is Campbellite patrimony;*[13] *prophetic criticism is harbinger of restoration.* Do you agree?" I asked them.

"I hardly understand it!" rejoined Chalice. "Maybe tell me about the mud again. Better start with the mud." At this, I gave another impressive sigh, and it seemed to me that Campbell's portrait smirked (slightly).

---

[13] I recognize that choice of this gendered term is unfortunate; it suits my intentions for this essay, but should not be read as suggesting that any (beneficial) Stone-Campbell inheritance is solely a gift from men (i.e., males). Nevertheless, an important voice in the prophetic critique I describe below is a *feminist* voice; in other words, feminist prophetic criticism is desperately needed in our congregations and at our universities.

"We are born into mud. A tree cannot move by itself, but with all its might must spread its branches wide and try to achieve its ordained height with tremendous effort in that one place on earth given to it by God. Likewise, I was born into a certain tradition, I have inherited a faith, and yet I desire to spread my branches wide, to drink in more sunlight than my dim corner of the forest allows. For our tradition to grow and thrive, we must be willing to learn from others." Chalice nodded, his pewter handle tilting back and forth. "What about inheritance then?"

"Well, it seems to me that *prophetic criticism* is our birthright; critique is in our Campbellite blood. Prophetic criticism[14] is a dynamic force that generated our Movement's inception; throughout our history, prophets have arisen to challenge the status quo.[15] But the

---

[14] What I intend by prophetic criticism is informed by Walter Brueggemann, *The Prophetic Imagination*, 2nd ed. (Minneapolis: Fortress Press, 2001). Prophetic criticism is critique of dominant narratives that obscure truth, grief, and freedom in a kind of "static triumphalism" *by an insider to the community*. While Brueggemann's intent is much broader, I want to apply his observations to my local faith tradition, i.e., Churches of Christ. He says, "The church will not have the power to act or believe until it recovers its tradition of faith and permits that tradition to be the primal way out of enculturation. This is not a cry for traditionalism but rather a judgment that the church has no business more pressing than the reappropriation of its memory in its full power and authenticity. And that is true among liberals who are too chic to remember and conservatives who have overlaid the faith memory with all kinds of hedges that smack of scientism and Enlightenment" (2). Within the Stone-Campbell heritage, prophetic critique can be an act of *energizing memory*, of "letting people see their own history in the light of God's freedom and his will for justice" (116), so that we might confront and grieve injustices and distortions of freedom in our history, beliefs, and practices.

[15] Consider Paul M. Blowers, "Neither Calvinists nor Arminians, but Simply Christians: The Stone-Campbell Movement as a Theological Resistance Movement," *Lexington Theological Quarterly* 35, no. 3 (September 2000): 133-154. At this point, Stone-Campbell archives become a vibrant source of *remembrance*. Among other issues, prophets have arisen (and are even now among us!) who challenge disunity, discrimination and racial injustices, exceptionalism, triumphalism in missions and evangelism, limitation and exclusion of women, inhospitable or hostile attitudes toward LGBT+ individuals, and especially, our traditional approach to reading and interpreting the Bible. Both the Restoration Principle and our inherited hermeneutics have been subjected to necessary critique. See discussion in Richard T. Hughes, *Reviving the Ancient Faith* (Grand Rapids, MI: William B. Eerdmans, 1996), 363-375; see also Thomas H. Olbricht, "Hermeneutics in the Churches of Christ," *Restoration Quarterly* 37, no. 1 (1995): 1-24. For a recent, helpful critique of literalist hermeneutics, see

prophetic voice is not a voice from outside; though they cry from the fringes, prophets are internal to the community and must do their prophetic work from inside. This is an important reason why I think it is necessary to stay: our congregations and universities foster cultures that learn to recognize and value the crucial importance of prophetic criticism only when the prophets stay and do their work. When prophets leave, they lose their voice and turn from prophet to cynic. Prophetic criticism is insider work."[16] Even as I spoke these words, I found myself wondering if (perhaps hoping that) Campbell would agree. Yet he sat unmoved, ever furrowed, piercing me with his glare. Chalice interrupted: "And what of the second clause, the part about restoration? Simplify your thesis; it's too thick to be useful."

"With others, I believe that restoration is not static, but ongoing and dynamic.[17] Restoration is not something our forbearers *did*, as if they then brushed themselves off and clasped hands for a job well done. Restoration is now, ever present, ever new. Here's another thick statement, thick like honey and I hope it sticks: The

---

Peter Enns, *The Bible Tells Me So: Why Defending Scripture Has Made Us Unable to Read It* (San Francisco: HarperOne, 2014). Also, for a recent challenge to incorporate better theological discourse within Churches of Christ, see Brad East, "Hooking In, Sitting Loose: A Call for Theology in the Churches of Christ," *Restoration Quarterly* 54, no. 4 (2012): 219-228. I also found this article to be a powerful, recent example from the mission field: Scott Mágkachi Sabóy, "A Brown Man's Burden: Critiquing an American Restorationist Discourse," *International Journal of The Sociology of Language* 2014, no. 229 (September 2014): 67-94. Make friends with your local Stone-Campbell archivist or historian for specific examples of prophetic criticism in our Movement's past and present.

[16] As Brueggemann argues, prophetic criticism is performed from the inside, as the Incarnation demonstrates: "The cross is the assurance that effective prophetic criticism is done not by an outsider but always by one who must embrace the grief, enter into the death, and know the pain of the criticized one." See Brueggemann, 99. Earlier, Brueggemann also asserts that, "The prophet is called to be a child of the tradition, one who has taken it seriously in the shaping of his or her own field of perception and system of language, who is so at home in that memory that the points of contact and incongruity with the situation of the church in culture can be discerned and articulated with proper urgency" (2).

[17] Consider the second-coming orientation of Barton Stone's restoration vision as described by Richard T. Hughes, "Reclaiming a Heritage," *Restoration Quarterly* 37, no. 3 (1995): 129-138.

Kingdom of Heaven is the reality of God's cosmic governance impinging on our present moment; peaceable, loving, just, merciful choices in the here and now *reveal* the challenging presence of God's kingdom both to ourselves and to others; in fact, the kingdom is only revealed in love for neighbor, and its reality is only ever enacted as we rush toward and love the others we encounter. Love reveals heaven's challenging presence among us, and it is the revelation of heaven that is *restoration's movement*: when heaven and the hope that God restores all things are revealed in our present moments, that is the restoration movement."[18]

Chalice had fallen asleep again. I glanced at Campbell: countenance like stone. The archive had righted itself. My thesis remained, scrawled on paper atop a low desk, beneath flickering fluorescents, thick as it had been at the beginning. But I swear, I heard Lindsay chanting from the archival boxes, with a deep and resonant *boom-lay, boom-lay, boom-lay, boom!* And he whispered, as one whispers to remind another of some forgotten thing:

> O prodigal son, O recreant daughter,
> When broken by the death of a child
> You called for the greybeard Campbellite elder,
> Who spoke as of old in the wild.
> His voice held echoes in the deep woods of Kentucky.
> He towered in apostolic state,
> While the portrait of Campbell emerged from the dark:
> That genius beautiful and great.
> And millennial trumpets poised, half lifted,
> Millennial trumpets that wait.[19]

Bibliography

Blowers, Paul M. "Neither Calvinists nor Arminians, but Simply Christians: The Stone-Campbell Movement as a Theological Resistance Movement." *Lexington Theological Quarterly* 35, no. 3 (September 2000): 133-154.

---

[18] Both language and concept here are informed by Disciples scholar Joe Jones, *A Grammar of Christian Faith* (Lanham, MD: Rowman and Littlefield, 2002), 2: 703-710.

[19] Lindsay, 175.

Brueggemann, Walter. *The Prophetic Imagination*, 2nd ed. Minneapolis: Fortress Press, 2001.

Campbell, Alexander. "The Gospel." *Millennial Harbinger* 36, no. 11 (November 1865): 516-517.

———. "The Third Epistle of Peter: To the Preachers and Rulers of Congregations." *The Christian Baptist* 2, no. 12 (July 1825): 243-47.

Campbell, Selina Huntington. *Home Life and Reminiscences of Alexander Campbell*. St. Louis: J. Burns, 1882.

East, Brad. "Hooking In, Sitting Loose: A Call for Theology in the Churches of Christ." *Restoration Quarterly* 54, no. 4 (2012): 219-228.

Enns, Peter. *The Bible Tells Me So: Why Defending Scripture Has Made Us Unable to Read It*. San Francisco: HarperOne, 2014.

Folks, Jeffrey. "Vachel Lindsay's Covenant with America." *Modern Age* 50, no. 4 (Fall 2008): 321-331.

Gresham, Charles R. "Lindsay, Vachel." In *Encyclopedia of the Stone-Campbell Movement*, edited by Douglas Foster, et al., 479-480. Grand Rapids, MI: William B. Eerdmans, 2004.

Hoshino, Tomihiro, Gavin Bantock, and Kyoko Oshima Bantock. *Journey of the Wind*. Tōkyō: Rippū Shobō, 1988.

Hughes, Richard T. *Reviving the Ancient Faith*. Grand Rapids, MI: William B. Eerdmans, 1996.

———. "Reclaiming a Heritage." *Restoration Quarterly* 37, no. 3 (1995): 129-138.

Jones, Joe. *A Grammar of Christian Faith*. 2 vols. Lanham, MD: Rowman and Littlefield, 2002.

Lindsay, Vachel. "Alexander Campbell." In *The Golden Whales of California*. New York: MacMillan, 1920.

Masters, Edgar Lee. *Vachel Lindsay: A Poet in America*. New York: Biblo and Tannen, 1969.

Olbricht, Thomas H. "Hermeneutics in the Churches of Christ." *Restoration Quarterly* 37, no. 1 (1995): 1-24.

Rothenburger, William Frederic. "Vachel Lindsay." *Shane Quarterly* 5, no. 2-3 (April 1944): 144-147.

Sabóy, Scott Mágkachi. "A Brown Man's Burden: Critiquing an American Restorationist Discourse." *International Journal of The Sociology of Language* 2014, no. 229 (September 2014): 67-94.

Wakefield, Olive Lindsay. "Vachel Lindsay, Disciple." *Shane Quarterly* 5, no. 2-3 (April 1944): 82-107.

If you enjoyed this book, please consider leaving a review or rating online at Amazon or other retailer.

For author news, other titles, new publications, and discount offers, subscribe to the Sulis International Publishing newsletter at [https://goo.gl/2SVDju]

Printed in Great Britain
by Amazon